The Insider's
Florida Bucket List

*A Full-Color Florida Travel Guide to Hidden Gems,
Must-See Spots and Local Secrets Only Insiders Know*

Mark Smith

ALL RIGHTS RESERVED

Copyright © 2025 Mark Smith

No part of this publication may be reproduced, distributed, or transmitted in any form or by any means, including photocopying, recording, or other electronic or mechanical methods, without the prior written permission of the author, except in the case of brief quotations used in reviews, articles, or scholarly work with proper attribution.

DISCLAIMER

This book is intended as a general guide for travelers and is provided for informational purposes only. While every effort has been made to ensure the accuracy of the information contained within, the author and publisher make no representations or warranties regarding the completeness, accuracy, or reliability of any information, services, or products mentioned.

Travel conditions, business hours, prices, and availability can change without notice. It is strongly recommended that readers verify information independently, particularly for time-sensitive details such as attraction hours, road closures, and event schedules.

The author and publisher disclaim any liability for any direct, indirect, incidental, or consequential damages that may result from the use of the information provided in this book.

HEALTH & SAFETY NOTICE

Travel involves inherent risks, and it is the responsibility of each traveler to assess their personal health and safety when engaging in activities mentioned in this guide. Readers should follow all local laws, regulations, and health guidelines, especially in relation to weather conditions, wildlife encounters, and outdoor activities.

TRADEMARKS & ACKNOWLEDGMENTS

All trademarks, logos, and brand names mentioned in this book are the property of their respective owners. References to specific businesses, attractions, or services are for informational purposes only and do not imply endorsement by the author or publisher.

Special thanks to all the local experts, businesses, and fellow travelers who provided insights and inspiration for this guide.

Contents

PREFACE — 10

INTRODUCTION — 11

Welcome to the Sunshine State — 11
A Quick Overview of Florida's Regions — 12
North Florida: Historic Charm and Natural Wonders — 12
Central Florida: The Heart of Theme Parks and Hidden Gems — 12
South Florida: Tropical Culture and Nightlife — 12
The Florida Keys: A Tropical Paradise — 12
How to Use This Guide — 13
How This Guide is Organized — 13
Planning Your Trip — 13
    Building Your Itinerary — 13
    Thematic Itineraries for Inspiration — 13
    Navigating the Regions — 13
    Alphabetical Index — 13

USING YOUR FLORIDA MAP — 15

What You'll See at First Glance — 15
Major Cities, Roads, and Access Points — 15
    Access Points — 16
Understanding the Icons and the Numbered Key — 16
    1. Icons — 16
    2. Numbered Key — 16
A Simple Map with a Big Impact — 17
Making the Most of It — 17

Part 1

NORTH FLORIDA — 19

Amelia Island — 20
1. Amelia Island Beaches — 20
2. Fort Clinch State Park — 20
3. Fernandina Beach Historic District — 21

Apalachicola — 21
4. Apalachicola Historic District — 21
5. St. George Island State Park — 22

Big Talbot Island — 22
6. Big Talbot Island (Boneyard Beach) — 22

Cape San Blas — 23
7. Cape San Blas Beaches — 23

Cedar Key — 23
8. Cedar Key Beaches — 23
9. Cedar Lakes Woods and Gardens — 25

Chiefland — 25
10. Devil's Den Prehistoric Spring — 25

DeLand — 26
11. DeLand's Stetson Mansion — 26
12. Old Spanish Sugar Mill (De Leon Springs) — 26

Falling Waters — 27
13. Falling Waters State Park — 27

Grayton Beach	27
14. Grayton Beach State Park	27
Homosassa	28
15. Three Sisters Springs	28
Milton	28
16. Blackwater River State Forest	28
Navarre	30
17. Navarre Beach	30
Pensacola	30
16. Pensacola Lighthouse and Museum	30
17. Pensacola Beach	31
18. Perdido Key	31
19. Gulf Islands National Seashore	31
St. Augustine	32
20. St. Augustine Historic District	32
21. Castillo de San Marcos National Monument	32
22. St. Augustine Lighthouse and Maritime Museum	33
Tallahassee Area	33
23. Wakulla Springs State Park	33
24. St. Marks Wildlife Refuge	34
25. Torreya State Park	34
Central Florida	**37**
Crystal River	38
26. Crystal River (Swim with Manatees)	38
Lake Placid	38
27. Lake Placid Murals	38
Merritt Island	39
28. Merritt Island Wildlife Refuge (Bioluminescence)	39
Mount Dora	39
29. Mount Dora Downtown	39
30. Mount Dora Scenic Boat Tours	41
Ocala	41
31. Silver Springs State Park	41
32. Juniper Springs Canoeing	42
33. Rainbow Springs Tubing	42
34. Ocala National Forest	42
Orlando	43
35. Walt Disney World Resort	43
36. Universal Studios Florida	43
37. LEGOLAND Florida Resort	44
38. SeaWorld Orlando	44
39. Gatorland	44
40. Harry P. Leu Gardens	46
Shark Valley (Everglades)	46
41. Shark Valley (Everglades Cycling and Tram Tours)	46
Tampa	47
42. Tampa Bay History Center	47
43. Historic Ybor City	47
Winter Park	48
44. Winter Park Scenic Boat Tour	48

Lake Wales	48
45. Bok Tower Gardens	48
Marianna	49
46. Florida Caverns State Park	49

South Florida — 51

Anna Maria Island	52
47. Anna Maria Island Beaches	52
Boca Grande	52
48. Gasparilla Island (Boca Grande)	52
Boynton Beach	53
49. Boynton Beach Oceanfront Park	53
Clearwater	53
50. Clearwater Beach	53
Coral Gables	55
51. Coral Gables Venetian Pool	55
Fort Lauderdale	55
51. Fort Lauderdale's Las Olas Boulevard	55
Fort Myers	56
52. Edison and Ford Winter Estates	56
53. Fort Myers Beach	56
Hollywood	56
54. Hollywood Beach Broadwalk	56
Key Biscayne	57
55. Key Biscayne Lighthouse	57
Lover's Key	57
56. Lover's Key State Park	57
Marco Island	58
57. Marco Island Beaches	58
Matlacha (Pine Island)	58
58. Matlacha Art District	58
Miami	60
59. Art Deco Historic District	60
60. Miami Beach and South Beach	60
Naples	61
61. Naples Pier and Beaches	61
62. Naples Botanical Garden	61
Sarasota	61
63. The Ringling Museum of Art	61
64. Sarasota Jungle Gardens	62
65. Siesta Key Beach	62
Solomon's Castle (Ona)	63
66. Solomon's Castle	63
Venice	63
67. Venice Beach (Shark Tooth Capital)	63
Everglades Region	63
68. Everglades National Park	63
69. Big Cypress National Preserve	64
70. Shark Valley (Everglades Cycling and Tram Tours)	64

Jupiter Area	**65**
71. Blowing Rocks Preserve	65
Caladesi Island	**65**
72. Caladesi Island State Park	65
Florida Keys	**67**
Big Pine Key	**68**
73. Big Pine Key (Key Deer Refuge)	68
74. Shark Tooth Hunting in the Keys	68
Cudjoe Key	**68**
74. Cudjoe Key Wildlife Refuge	68
Dry Tortugas	**69**
75. Dry Tortugas National Park	69
Islamorada	**69**
76. Islamorada (Sportfishing Capital)	69
77. Robbie's Marina (Feed the Tarpon)	71
78. Kayaking Through Mangroves	71
79. Snorkeling the Florida Keys Wreck Trail	71
John Pennekamp Coral Reef State Park (Key Largo)	**72**
80. John Pennekamp Coral Reef State Park	72
Key Largo	**72**
81. Key Largo Coral Reef State Park	72
82. Kayaking Through Mangroves	73
83. Snorkeling the Florida Keys Wreck Trail	73
84. Shark Tooth Hunting in the Keys	73
Key West	**74**
85. Key West and Mallory Square	74
86. Ernest Hemingway House	74
87. Fort Zachary Taylor Historic State Park	76
Little Torch Key	**76**
88. Little Torch Key (Secluded Escape)	76
Long Key	**77**
89. Long Key State Park	77
Marathon	**77**
90. Marathon's Turtle Hospital	77
91. Bioluminescent Kayaking	77
92. Kayaking Through Mangroves	78
Sugarloaf Key	**78**
93. Sugarloaf Key Bat Tower	78

Part 2

Natural Paradises	**81**
Chiefland	**82**
94. Manatee Springs State Park	82
Copeland	**82**
95. Fakahatchee Strand Preserve State Park	82

Gainesville	82
96. Devil's Millhopper Geological State Park	82
Islamorada	83
97. Windley Key Fossil Reef Geological State Park	83
Jupiter	83
98. Blowing Rocks Preserve	83
Live Oak	85
99. Peacock Springs State Park	85
Ocala National Forest	85
100. Juniper Prairie Wilderness	85
St. Petersburg	85
101. Egmont Key State Park	85
White Springs	86
102. Big Shoals State Park	86
Dog Island (Gulf Coast)	86
103. Dog Island	86
Blue Spring (Orange City)	87
104. Blue Spring State Park	87
Devil's Den (Williston)	87
105. Devil's Den Prehistoric Spring	87
St. Vincent Island (Apalachicola)	88
106. St. Vincent Island	88
Cayo Costa (Pine Island Sound)	88
107. Cayo Costa State Park	88

Cultural and Historic Sites	**91**
Cedar Key	92
108. Cedar Key Museum State Park	92
Cape Romano	92
109. The Dome Houses of Cape Romano	92
Ellenton	93
110. Madira Bickel Mound State Archaeological Site	93
Bradenton	93
111. De Soto National Memorial	93
Ona	94
112. Solomon's Castle	94
Micanopy	94
113. Micanopy Historic District	94
Unique and Curious Spots	**97**
Dunedin	98
114. Honeymoon Island Pet Beach	98
Estero	98
115. The Old Corkscrew Golf Club	98
Riviera Beach	99
116. Peanut Island	99
Seaside	99
117. Seaside Scenic Town	99

Part 3

Planning the ultimate family getaway? — 101

Family-Friendly Adventures — 102
- 1-Day Itinerary — 102
- 3-Day Itinerary — 102
- 7-Day Itinerary — 103
- General Tips for Families — 105

Romantic Getaways — 105
- 1-Day Itinerary — 106
- 3-Day Itinerary — 106
- 7-Day Itinerary — 107
- General Tips for Romantic Getaways — 108

Cultural and Historic Road Trips — 108
- 1-Day Trip — 108
- 3-Day Trip — 109
- 7-Day Trip — 110
- General Tips for a Cultural and Historical Road Trip — 111

ENJOYED THIS GUIDE? YOUR REVIEW HELPS! — 114
- Unlock Your Free Bonuses! — 114

Preface

Hi there, fellow traveler!

If you're holding this book, chances are you're dreaming about Florida—or maybe you've already booked your trip and you're counting down the days. Either way, I get it. I really do. **Florida has this magnetic pull, doesn't it?** The promise of endless sunshine, turquoise waters, and a mix of thrills and tranquility. Whether it's your first visit or your tenth, **you want this trip to be unforgettable.** And let's face it, when you're coming from as far away as New York, London, or even Canada (like so many of the **130+ million visitors we welcome annually**), the stakes feel high. **You want a guide that doesn't just scratch the surface but helps you really experience Florida.**

That's where I come in. **My name is Mark Smith, born and raised in Sarasota, right on Florida's Gulf Coast.** This book isn't from a big-name publisher with glossy photos and a marketing budget the size of a theme park. Nope. **It's just me, someone who loves this state and knows it inside out, sharing everything I've learned over the years.**

Sure, you won't find pages filled with perfectly lit photos of beaches and palm trees here. (I figured you've already seen plenty of those on Instagram.) Instead, **I've packed this guide with what I think matters more—practical tips, hidden gems, and local insights you won't find in the usual tourist brochures.** Want to know where to get the **best key lime pie that isn't a tourist trap?** Or the **quiet spot to catch a sunset that locals love but guidebooks ignore?** That's the kind of stuff you'll find here.

Because **I know what you're looking for: a guide that makes you feel like you've got a friend in Florida.** Someone who understands that this isn't just another trip for you—it's an adventure, a chance to make memories, and maybe even discover a side of Florida you didn't know existed.

So, let's get started. **Together, we'll make sure your time in the Sunshine State is everything you hoped for—and then some.**

Mark Smith

Safe travels,

Introduction

Welcome to the Sunshine State

Hey there, and welcome to Florida—where the sun always shines, the water sparkles, and every day feels like a new adventure waiting to happen. Let me ask you: what brought you here? Maybe it's the call of sandy beaches, the thrill of theme parks, or just the idea of escaping the ordinary. Whatever it is, I'm so glad you're here, because this place has a little bit of magic for everyone. Growing up in Florida, I've discovered that no matter how many times you visit, there's always something new, unexpected, and unforgettable just around the corner. Are you ready to explore?

This isn't your typical guidebook filled with dry lists and directions. Think of it as a local friend walking you through the Sunshine State, pointing out the must-sees, the hidden gems, and the little details that make Florida so special. I'll take you to the places where memories are made—the kind of spots you'll be telling stories about for years to come. Whether you're here for a quick getaway or planning the trip of a lifetime, this guide is your key to experiencing Florida like someone who truly knows and loves it.

So, what can you expect? Well, let's start with options. Do you dream of turquoise waters and palm-lined beaches? Or maybe you're craving adrenaline-fueled adventures in world-famous theme parks? Looking for a romantic escape or curious about Florida's fascinating history? Whatever your idea of the perfect trip is, you'll find it here. From seasonal tips to tailored itineraries and insider advice, this guide is packed with everything you need to make your Florida adventure unforgettable.

Let me share a little secret with you. Florida, for me, it's the way the salty breeze hits your face on a sunset sail, or how the mangroves whisper as you paddle through their quiet waters.

I still remember summers spent exploring hidden trails and stumbling upon tiny islands that felt like they belonged to another world. It's that sense of wonder I want you to feel as you flip through these pages and, more importantly, when you set out on your own journey.

So, what do you say? Let's dive in together, uncover the beauty of this incredible place, and make your Florida story one you'll never forget. You're going to love it here—I promise.

A Quick Overview of Florida's Regions

Florida isn't just a state—it's a vibrant mosaic of cultures, landscapes, and experiences. From the Spanish-inspired streets of St. Augustine to the tropical charm of the Florida Keys, each region has its own story to tell. Planning your trip starts with understanding these diverse areas, so let's dive into what makes each corner of Florida unique.

North Florida: Historic Charm and Natural Wonders

Looking for a slower pace and a touch of history? North Florida has you covered. Explore **St. Augustine**, the nation's oldest city, with its cobblestone streets and centuries-old forts. Or immerse yourself in nature at **Wakulla Springs**, home to some of the clearest waters in the state. This region is where history meets the great outdoors, offering a perfect blend of learning and leisure.

Central Florida: The Heart of Theme Parks and Hidden Gems

This is where the magic happens—literally! From **Walt Disney World** to **Universal Studios**, Central Florida is the epicenter of family-friendly fun. But there's more here than just roller coasters. Take a stroll through **Mount Dora**, a charming town known for its antique shops and lakefront views, or visit **Leu Gardens** in Orlando for a tranquil escape.

South Florida: Tropical Culture and Nightlife

Vibrant and dynamic, South Florida is where the party meets paradise. In **Miami**, you'll find a cultural melting pot with Latin-inspired flavors, world-class art, and lively nightlife. If you're looking for something more serene, head to **Naples** or **Fort Lauderdale** for sun-soaked beaches and peaceful coastal retreats. This region perfectly balances energy and relaxation.

The Florida Keys: A Tropical Paradise

Welcome to the Keys, where the water is impossibly blue and life moves at an island pace. Snorkel through coral reefs at **John Pennekamp Coral Reef State Park**, savor fresh seafood in **Key West**, or simply watch the sun melt into the horizon during one of the Keys' legendary sunsets. It's a slice of paradise you won't want to leave.

No matter where you begin your journey, every region in Florida has something unforgettable to offer. Maybe you'll be enchanted by the history of the north, the magic of the center, the vibrancy of the south, or the tranquility of the Keys. Wherever your heart takes you, I'll be here to guide you every step of the way. So, where will you start?

How to Use This Guide

Planning a trip to Florida should feel exciting, not overwhelming. That's why I created this guide—to be your go-to travel buddy, whether you're sneaking away for a weekend or diving into a week-long adventure. Think of it as that one friend who always knows the best spots, hidden gems, and practical tips to make every trip feel special. With carefully curated itineraries, regional highlights, and seasonal recommendations, this guide will help you craft a trip that's as unique as you are.

How This Guide is Organized

I've broken everything down into easy-to-navigate sections to make your planning as smooth as possible:

- **Regional Overviews:** Get a feel for what makes each part of Florida special, from North Florida's historic charm to the tropical magic of the Keys.
- **Thematic Itineraries:** Whether you're a history buff, nature lover, or beach bum, find pre-planned itineraries ranging from 1 to 7 days.
- **Hidden Gems:** Skip the tourist traps and explore the lesser-known spots that only locals know about.

- **BONUS - Seasonal Highlights:** Discover what's best to see and do in Florida during spring, summer, fall, and winter, so you can time your visit perfectly. You can download them by scanning the QR code at the end of this book.

Planning Your Trip

Building Your Itinerary

Each destination comes with practical information, local tips, and suggested activities. Use the regional maps and thematic itineraries to design a trip that matches your interests.

Thematic Itineraries for Inspiration

- **Only have a day?** Pick a 1-day itinerary to hit the highlights.
- **Got more time?** Dive into a 7-day plan for an immersive experience packed with variety.

Navigating the Regions

If you already know where you want to go, head to the corresponding regional section to discover top attractions, hidden gems, and practical advice.

Alphabetical Index

Need to find a specific spot quickly? Flip to the index at the back of the book to locate destinations in no time.

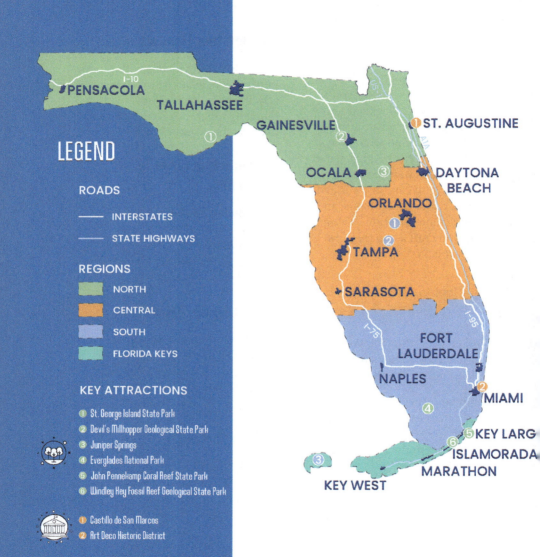

Using Your Florida Map

Let's be real—planning a trip can be overwhelming, especially when you're working with a state as diverse and exciting as Florida. But don't worry—you've got this map, and trust me, it's going to make things a whole lot easier. Whether you're plotting a coast-to-coast road trip or just trying to figure out the best way to hop from Orlando's theme parks to Miami's beaches, this map has you covered.

What You'll See at First Glance

Take a moment to soak it all in. You'll notice that Florida is divided into **four regions, each color-coded for easy navigation**:

- **North Florida (Light Green):** History and nature come together, with iconic spots like St. Augustine and the peaceful landscapes of Wakulla Springs.
- **Central Florida (Soft Orange):** Theme parks, natural springs, and charming towns like Ocala await.
- **South Florida (Pastel Blue):** Think white-sand beaches, vibrant cities like Miami, and the cultural richness of Naples and Fort Lauderdale.
- **Florida Keys (Bright Turquoise):** Where tropical vibes reign supreme, from Key Largo's coral reefs to Key West's famous sunsets.

Major Cities, Roads, and Access Points

Navigating Florida is easy once you know the major cities and access routes. The **bold city labels** show key hubs, perfect for overnight stays or starting your next adventure:

- **North Florida:** Tallahassee, Pensacola, St. Augustine, Gainesville.
- **Central Florida:** Orlando, Tampa, Ocala, Daytona Beach.
- **South Florida:** Miami, Naples, Fort Lauderdale, Sarasota.
- **Florida Keys:** Key Largo, Islamorada, Marathon, Key West.

Access Points

On the map, you'll notice **key highways and interstates** that act as primary access routes to major regions and attractions:

- **I-95:** The main route along Florida's east coast, connecting Jacksonville to Miami.
- **I-75:** Stretching from Gainesville down to Naples and Miami, making it ideal for cross-regional travel.
- **I-10:** Perfect for exploring North Florida, running from Pensacola to Jacksonville.
- **US-1:** Your main access point to the Florida Keys.
- **A1A:** The scenic route for those who want a coastal view, stretching from St. Augustine to Daytona Beach.

Understanding the Icons and the Numbered Key

You've probably noticed two things: icons and numbers. These work together to guide you to Florida's **key attractions**, which are listed in the legend on the bottom left of the map. Here's how to read them:

1. Icons

The three icons represent key attraction categories: **Historic/Cultural Landmarks** (forts, museums, architecture), **Nature/Outdoor Activities** (parks, springs, wildlife), and **Theme Parks/Unique Experiences** (theme parks, quirky destinations, offbeat adventures). Use them to plan your ideal trip! These symbols are your fast-pass to understanding what type of adventure awaits, whether it's hiking through natural wonders or soaking up some history.

2. Numbered Key

Each key attraction on the map is marked with a corresponding number. For example:

- **1 - St. George Island State Park:** Located in North Florida, perfect for beach lovers and nature seekers.
- **3 - Juniper Springs (Ocala):** A hidden gem offering crystal-clear spring water and scenic kayaking routes.
- **6 - Dry Tortugas National Park:** Situated off the coast of Key West, offering snorkeling and fort tours.

Simply match the number on the map to the legend, and you'll quickly identify what type of adventure awaits.

A Simple Map with a Big Impact

This map is intentionally **clean and clutter-free**, giving you a broad view without overwhelming you with too much information. But when you're ready to dive deeper, **scan the QR code at the bottom of the page to download the expanded and printable A2 map**. It includes even more destinations and details, perfect for planning a truly comprehensive Florida trip.

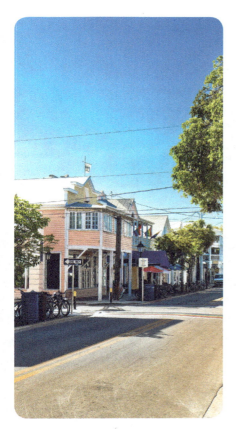

Making the Most of It

1. **Plan your route:** Use the cities, roads, and regions to map out your journey.
2. **Icons and key attractions:** Quickly identify nature spots, historic landmarks, or unique experiences with the help of the legend.
3. **Upgrade when needed:** The basic map is perfect for overview planning, but for the finer details, the expanded digital version has you covered.

So, where will your adventure begin? Whether you're following major highways or venturing off the beaten path, this map will be your guide to discovering the Sunshine State's best-kept secrets. Grab your map, scan the QR code, and get ready to hit the road—Florida is waiting!

https://drive.google.com/drive/folders/1xoquaFj3FEgKLdCg-C6CTT4z8A5oSsKz-?usp=drive_link

Part 1

Florida Bucket List Destinations

NORTH FLORIDA

Amelia Island

1. Amelia Island Beaches

Location: Amelia Island, North Florida

Address: Amelia Island, FL 32034

Description:

Amelia Island Beaches offer 13 miles of pristine coastline, making it a haven for nature lovers and beach enthusiasts. Known for its uncrowded shores, this tranquil destination is perfect for relaxation and reconnecting with nature.

Activities and Attractions:

Enjoy sunbathing, swimming, and shell hunting along the sandy shores. Outdoor enthusiasts can explore nearby hiking and biking trails or take a horseback ride at sunrise. Kayaking through the island's scenic marshes is another unforgettable experience.

Practical Information:

Open year-round, but the best time to visit is spring and fall for pleasant weather. There's no admission fee for public beach access, and ample parking is available.

Local Tips:

Arrive early to secure a peaceful spot on the sand. Don't miss a meal at one of the nearby seafood shacks serving fresh catch of the day!

2. Fort Clinch State Park

Location: Amelia Island, North Florida

Address: 2601 Atlantic Ave, Fernandina Beach, FL 32034

Description:

Fort Clinch State Park combines history and natural beauty in one unforgettable destination. The well-preserved 19th-century fort offers a fascinating glimpse into Civil War-era life, surrounded by lush landscapes and coastal views.

Activities and Attractions:

Tour the historic fort with costumed interpreters bringing the past to life. Hike or bike through the park's scenic trails, or enjoy fishing, swimming, and shelling along the shoreline. The wildlife spotting opportunities, including deer and shorebirds, are excellent.

Practical Information:

The park is open daily from 8:00 AM until sunset. Fort access requires an additional fee of $2.50 per person on top of the $6 vehicle entrance fee. Guided tours are available on weekends.

Local Tips:

Visit during a reenactment event for a unique historical experience. Don't forget your camera to capture the stunning views from the fort's ramparts!

3. Fernandina Beach Historic District

Location: Amelia Island, North Florida

Address: Centre Street, Fernandina Beach, FL 32034

Description:

Step back in time in the Fernandina Beach Historic District, a charming area known for its Victorian-era architecture, cobblestone streets, and vibrant local culture. This quaint downtown is the heart of Amelia Island's history and charm.

Activities and Attractions:

Stroll along Centre Street to explore boutique shops, art galleries, and cozy cafes. Visit the Amelia Island Museum of History to learn about the area's fascinating past. Don't miss a scenic river cruise to see the historic waterfront and local wildlife.

Practical Information:

The district is accessible year-round, with many shops and attractions open daily. Free parking is available in several designated areas. Special events, like the annual Shrimp Festival, add extra excitement.

Local Tips:

Arrive early to avoid crowds and enjoy a leisurely breakfast at a local café. Sunset views from the marina are breathtaking, so plan to stay into the evening!

Apalachicola

4. Apalachicola Historic District

Location: Apalachicola, North Florida

Address: Downtown Apalachicola, FL 32320

Description:

The Apalachicola Historic District is a hidden gem steeped in maritime history and Southern charm. With over 900 historic buildings, this quaint area showcases beautifully preserved 19th-century architecture and a vibrant connection to Florida's past.

Activities and Attractions:

Wander through charming streets lined with historic homes, antique shops, and local boutiques. Stop by the John Gorrie Museum to learn about the invention of air conditioning. Don't miss the waterfront, where fishing boats unload fresh seafood daily.

Practical Information:

The district is free to explore year-round, with most shops and attractions open during standard business hours. Many restaurants serve fresh Apalachicola oysters, a local specialty.

Local Tips:

Visit during the annual Florida Seafood Festival for a lively celebration of local flavors and culture. For a quieter experience, explore early in the morning when the streets are calm and peaceful.

5. St. George Island State Park

Location: St. George Island, North Florida

Address: 1900 E Gulf Beach Dr, St. George Island, FL 32328

Description:

St. George Island State Park is a serene coastal retreat offering nine miles of unspoiled beaches, pristine dunes, and breathtaking Gulf views. It's a paradise for nature lovers and outdoor enthusiasts seeking tranquility.

Activities and Attractions:

Relax on the sandy shores, perfect for sunbathing and swimming. Explore hiking trails winding through lush pine forests or enjoy birdwatching and spotting coastal wildlife. Kayaking and paddleboarding in the clear waters are popular activities.

Practical Information:

The park is open daily from 8:00 AM to sunset. Admission costs $6 per vehicle. Seasonal camping and picnic areas are available for visitors looking to extend their stay.

Local Tips:

Visit in the early morning or evening to avoid crowds and experience stunning sunrises or sunsets. Bring bug spray during warmer months and a picnic to enjoy at one of the shaded pavilions.

Big Talbot Island

6. Big Talbot Island (Boneyard Beach)

Location: Big Talbot Island, North Florida

Address: 12157 Heckscher Dr, Jacksonville, FL 32226

Description:

Big Talbot Island's Boneyard Beach is a unique natural wonder, famous for its striking driftwood-strewn shoreline. This otherworldly landscape offers a mix of beauty and mystery, making it a must-visit for nature photographers and explorers.

Activities and Attractions:

Explore the beach to see weathered trees sculpted by the elements. Hiking and biking trails wind through the island's maritime forest, offering scenic views of Nassau Sound. Kayaking and birdwatching are popular activities in this serene environment.

Practical Information:

The park is open daily from 8:00 AM to sunset. Admission is $3 per vehicle. Wear sturdy shoes for walking along the beach, as the terrain can be uneven.

Local Tips:

Visit during low tide for the best access to Boneyard Beach. Pack a camera to capture the dramatic driftwood formations, and enjoy a quiet picnic in one of the park's shaded areas.

Cape San Blas

7. Cape San Blas Beaches

Location: Cape San Blas, North Florida

Address: Cape San Blas Rd, Port St. Joe, FL 32456

Description:

Cape San Blas Beaches offer miles of pristine, uncrowded shoreline perfect for a peaceful getaway. With sugar-white sand and clear Gulf waters, this destination is ideal for those seeking relaxation and natural beauty.

Activities and Attractions:

Enjoy swimming, paddleboarding, and snorkeling in the calm waters. Take a leisurely stroll along the shore or search for seashells. Outdoor enthusiasts can explore the nearby St. Joseph Peninsula State Park, known for its hiking trails and wildlife.

Practical Information:

The beaches are open year-round with no admission fees. Parking is available in several designated areas. Summer is the most popular season, but spring and fall offer a quieter experience with pleasant weather.

Local Tips:

Bring a picnic and stay to watch the sunset, as Cape San Blas is famous for its spectacular evening skies. Keep an eye out for dolphins, which are frequently spotted close to shore.

Cedar Key

8. Cedar Key Beaches

Location: Cedar Key, North Florida

Address: 192 2nd St, Cedar Key, FL 32625

Description:

Cedar Key Beaches are a quaint and peaceful escape, perfect for soaking up small-town coastal charm. The calm waters and scenic views make it an ideal spot for relaxation and nature appreciation.

Activities and Attractions:

Enjoy kayaking, paddleboarding, or simply sunbathing on the shore. Take a stroll along the waterfront and explore local seafood restaurants and shops. Birdwatching enthusiasts will appreciate the variety of species in the area.

Practical Information:

The beaches are free and accessible year-round, with nearby parking available. Spring and fall are the best times to visit for pleasant weather and fewer crowds.

Local Tips:

Plan your visit around sunset for stunning views over the Gulf. Don't forget to sample fresh seafood at one of the local eateries, especially the famous Cedar Key clams.

DeLand

Evening photo of the historic Volusia County Courthouse and fountain pool in DeLand, Florida

Shutterstock / SEALANDSKYPHOTO

9. Cedar Lakes Woods and Gardens

Location: Cedar Key area, North Florida

Address: 4990 NE 180th Ave, Williston, FL 32696

Description:
Cedar Lakes Woods and Gardens is a lush botanical oasis filled with cascading waterfalls, koi ponds, and vibrant flowers. This hidden gem is perfect for nature lovers and photographers.

Activities and Attractions:
Wander along picturesque trails, admire unique garden landscapes, and relax by the serene ponds. Wildlife enthusiasts can spot various bird species and colorful butterflies.

Practical Information:
Open Wednesday through Sunday, from 9:30 AM to 4:30 PM. Admission is $12 for adults and $7 for children. Pets are welcome but must be leashed.

Local Tips:
Wear comfortable shoes for walking the trails and bring a hat for shade. Early mornings are the best time for a peaceful visit and vibrant photography opportunities.

Chiefland

10. Devil's Den Prehistoric Spring

Location: Chiefland, North Florida

Address: 5390 NE 180th Ave, Williston, FL 32696

Description:
Devil's Den Prehistoric Spring is a breathtaking underground natural wonder. This crystal-clear spring, located inside a karst cave, offers a unique opportunity to snorkel or dive in a setting unlike any other in Florida.

Activities and Attractions:
Snorkel or scuba dive to explore the spring's mesmerizing waters and admire its prehistoric rock formations. On the surface, enjoy a relaxing picnic or explore the nearby nature trails. Equipment rentals and lessons are available for beginners.

Practical Information:
The spring is open daily, but reservations are required for all activities. Snorkeling costs $25 per person, and diving fees vary. Guests must be at least 18 years old or accompanied by a guardian.

Local Tips:
Arrive early to beat the crowds, as space is limited. Bring an underwater camera to capture the stunning views, and wear a wetsuit for comfort in the cool 72°F water.

DeLand

11. DeLand's Stetson Mansion

Location: DeLand, North Florida

Address: 1031 Camphor Ln, DeLand, FL 32720

Description:

Stetson Mansion, Florida's first luxury home, is a stunning example of Gilded Age architecture. Built in 1886 by hat maker John B. Stetson, this meticulously restored mansion showcases intricate woodwork and stained glass windows.

Activities and Attractions:

Take a guided tour to explore the mansion's luxurious rooms, learn about its fascinating history, and admire the unique blend of architectural styles. Seasonal decorations make it especially enchanting during the holidays.

Practical Information:

Tours are available by reservation only and cost $30-$40 per person. The mansion is open year-round, with varying schedules depending on the season.

Local Tips:

Book your tour in advance, as spots fill quickly. Wear comfortable shoes, as the tour involves walking through multiple rooms and levels.

12. Old Spanish Sugar Mill (De Leon Springs)

Location: De Leon Springs State Park, DeLand, North Florida

Address: 601 Ponce de Leon Blvd, De Leon Springs, FL 32130

Description:

The Old Spanish Sugar Mill offers a unique dining experience where visitors can make their own pancakes at their table. Located in De Leon Springs State Park, it combines history, fun, and great food.

Activities and Attractions:

Enjoy creating pancakes with a variety of batters and toppings. After dining, explore the park's natural spring for swimming, canoeing, or hiking along scenic trails.

Practical Information:

The Sugar Mill is open daily from 9:00 AM to 2:00 PM and operates on a first-come, first-served basis. Admission to the state park is $6 per vehicle, and the pancake meal costs $6-$8 per person.

Local Tips:

Arrive early to avoid long waits, especially on weekends. Bring a swimsuit to enjoy the refreshing spring after your meal.

Falling Waters

13. Falling Waters State Park

Location: Chipley, North Florida

Address: 1130 State Park Rd, Chipley, FL 32428

Description:

Falling Waters State Park is home to Florida's tallest waterfall, where water cascades 73 feet into a deep sinkhole. Surrounded by lush forests and serene trails, it's a picturesque destination for nature enthusiasts.

Activities and Attractions:

Hike along scenic trails leading to the waterfall and explore the park's unique geological features, including sinkholes and caves. Enjoy picnicking, birdwatching, and fishing in the park's small lake. A campsite is also available for overnight stays.

Practical Information:

The park is open daily from 8:00 AM to sunset. Admission costs $5 per vehicle. Camping fees start at $18 per night, and reservations are recommended during peak seasons.

Local Tips:

Visit after heavy rains to see the waterfall at its most impressive. Wear sturdy shoes for hiking, as some trails can be uneven. Don't miss the butterfly garden, a hidden gem near the park entrance.

Grayton Beach

14. Grayton Beach State Park

Location: Grayton Beach, North Florida

Address: 357 Main Park Rd, Santa Rosa Beach, FL 32459

Description:

Grayton Beach State Park is a coastal gem featuring sugar-white sands, emerald-green waters, and scenic dune lakes. Perfect for a laid-back retreat, it's one of the most pristine and picturesque spots in Florida.

Activities and Attractions:

Relax on the beach, swim in the clear Gulf waters, or kayak in Western Lake, one of the state's rare coastal dune lakes. Hiking and biking trails weave through pine flatwoods, offering incredible views of the park's natural beauty.

Practical Information:

The park is open daily from 8:00 AM to sunset. Admission is $5 per vehicle. Campsites and cabins are available for overnight stays, but reservations are highly recommended, especially during peak seasons.

Local Tips:

Visit early in the morning for the most peaceful beach experience. Don't forget your camera to capture the stunning sunrise over the Gulf. For lunch, check out the charming restaurants in nearby Grayton Beach village.

Homosassa

15. Three Sisters Springs

Location: Crystal River, North Florida

Address: 601 Three Sisters Springs Trail, Crystal River, FL 34429

Description:

Three Sisters Springs is a haven for manatees and a paradise for nature lovers. With crystal-clear waters surrounded by lush greenery, it's one of Florida's most iconic natural springs.

Activities and Attractions:

Kayak, paddleboard, or swim in the refreshing waters. In winter, observe manatees in their natural habitat as they seek the warm spring waters. The boardwalk provides excellent views of the springs for non-swimmers.

Practical Information:

The springs are open daily, but access is by shuttle or kayak only. Entry fees vary based on activities, with swimming requiring a separate permit. Winter is the best time for manatee spotting.

Local Tips:

Arrive early for parking and quieter experiences. Rent a kayak to explore at your own pace and bring a waterproof camera for underwater photos of the springs.

Milton

16. Blackwater River State Forest

Location: Milton, North Florida

Address: 11650 Munson Hwy, Milton, FL 32570

Description:

Blackwater River State Forest is a natural retreat offering serene rivers, towering longleaf pines, and diverse wildlife. Known as a paddler's paradise, it's perfect for outdoor enthusiasts.

Activities and Attractions:

Enjoy canoeing or kayaking along the Blackwater River, famous for its sandy white banks and crystal-clear waters. Hike or bike the forest's trails, and try fishing or picnicking in designated areas.

Practical Information:

The forest is open year-round, with free access to most areas. Some campgrounds and trailheads may have small fees. Spring and fall are ideal for outdoor activities.

Local Tips:

Bring water shoes for paddling and explore less-trafficked trails for a peaceful hike. Check out the Juniper Lake area for a picturesque fishing spot.

Navarre Beach

Aerial view of Navarre Beach Florida Water Tower on the Gulf of Mexico on a sunny summer day

Shutterstock / Brenda Popovitz

Navarre

17. Navarre Beach

Location: Navarre, North Florida

Address: Navarre Beach, FL 32566

Description:

Navarre Beach is a serene, family-friendly destination with soft white sands and emerald-green waters. It's often referred to as "Florida's Most Relaxing Place."

Activities and Attractions:

Swim, sunbathe, or snorkel in the calm Gulf waters. Visit the Navarre Beach Marine Park for interactive exhibits or take a stroll along the pier, one of the longest in Florida.

Practical Information:

The beach is open year-round with no entry fees. Parking is free and widely available. Summer is the most popular time to visit, but spring and fall offer equally enjoyable weather with fewer crowds.

Local Tips:

Plan a visit to the Sea Turtle Conservation Center to learn about local marine life. For a quieter experience, explore the eastern end of the beach, away from the main public access.

Pensacola

16. Pensacola Lighthouse and Museum

Location: Pensacola, North Florida

Address: 2081 Radford Blvd, Pensacola, FL 32508

Description:

The Pensacola Lighthouse and Museum offers panoramic views of the Gulf Coast and a glimpse into maritime history. This 1859 lighthouse is one of the area's most iconic landmarks.

Activities and Attractions:

Climb the 177 steps to the top for stunning views, visit the museum to learn about the lighthouse's history, and explore the keeper's quarters. The site is also famous for ghost tours and paranormal investigations.

Practical Information:

Open daily from 9:00 AM to 5:00 PM. Admission is $8 for adults and $4 for children. Visitors must be at least 44 inches tall to climb the lighthouse.

Local Tips:

Visit at sunset for breathtaking views. Wear comfortable shoes for the climb and don't miss the nearby Naval Aviation Museum.

17. Pensacola Beach

Location: Pensacola Beach, North Florida

Address: Via de Luna Dr, Pensacola Beach, FL 32561

Description:

Pensacola Beach is a lively destination with powdery white sands and clear turquoise waters. Known for its vibrant atmosphere, it's perfect for families, couples, and solo travelers.

Activities and Attractions:

Relax on the beach, swim, or snorkel in the Gulf's calm waters. Explore the Pensacola Beach Boardwalk for dining, shopping, and live music. Water sports like paddleboarding and parasailing are popular here.

Practical Information:

The beach is open year-round with no admission fee. Ample parking is available, though it can fill up quickly during peak season.

Local Tips:

Arrive early to secure parking and a prime spot on the beach. For a quieter experience, head to the eastern end of the island.

18. Perdido Key

Location: Perdido Key, North Florida

Address: Perdido Key Dr, Perdido Key, FL 32507

Description:

Perdido Key offers a serene escape with miles of uncrowded beaches and natural beauty. It's an ideal spot for those seeking relaxation and a connection to nature.

Activities and Attractions:

Swim, fish, or paddleboard in the clear Gulf waters. Explore the Big Lagoon State Park nearby for hiking, birdwatching, and kayaking through tranquil waters.

Practical Information:

The beaches are open year-round, and parking is free in most areas. Summer is popular, but spring and fall provide equally pleasant weather with fewer crowds.

Local Tips:

Pack a picnic to enjoy on the beach and stay late to witness the stunning Gulf sunsets. Look for dolphins playing near the shore!

19. Gulf Islands National Seashore

Location: Pensacola and surrounding areas, North Florida

Address: 1801 Gulf Breeze Pkwy, Gulf Breeze, FL 32563

Description:

Gulf Islands National Seashore is a protected coastal area offering pristine beaches, historic sites, and abundant wildlife. It's perfect for nature lovers and history buffs alike.

Activities and Attractions:

Hike scenic trails, snorkel in crystal-clear waters, or explore historic Fort Pickens. Birdwatching and photography opportunities abound in this breathtaking setting.

Practical Information:

Open daily from sunrise to sunset. Entrance fees are $25 per vehicle for a seven-day pass. Campgrounds and picnic areas are available with advance reservations.

Local Tips:

Visit early in the morning for cooler temperatures and fewer crowds. Bring binoculars to spot wildlife, including sea turtles and nesting birds.

St. Augustine

20. St. Augustine Historic District

Location: St. Augustine, North Florida

Address: Historic Downtown St. Augustine, FL 32084

Description:

The St. Augustine Historic District is a captivating blend of history, culture, and charm. Known as the nation's oldest city, its cobblestone streets and colonial-era architecture transport visitors back in time.

Activities and Attractions:

Explore landmarks like Flagler College, the Oldest Wooden School House, and the vibrant St. George Street filled with shops and restaurants. Take a guided trolley or walking tour to learn about the area's rich history.

Practical Information:

The district is free to explore, with most attractions open daily. Parking can be limited, so consider using public lots or the Old Town Trolley for easier access.

Local Tips:

Visit in the evening for a magical ambiance under the city's historic lights. Don't miss the annual Nights of Lights festival during the holiday season.

21. Castillo de San Marcos National Monument

Location: St. Augustine, North Florida

Address: 1 S Castillo Dr, St. Augustine, FL 32084

Description:

Castillo de San Marcos, a 17th-century Spanish fort, is a symbol of St. Augustine's colonial past. Its coquina walls and stunning waterfront location make it a must-see for history enthusiasts.

Activities and Attractions:

Take a self-guided or ranger-led tour to explore the fort's rooms, cannons, and breathtaking views of Matanzas Bay. Historical reenactments and cannon firings occur regularly.

Practical Information:

The fort is open daily from 9:00 AM to 5:00 PM. Admission is $15 per adult, free for children under 16. The America the Beautiful pass is accepted.

Local Tips:

Arrive early to avoid crowds and bring sunscreen for outdoor areas. The sunrise view from the fort is especially memorable.

22. St. Augustine Lighthouse and Maritime Museum

Location: Anastasia Island, St. Augustine, North Florida

Address: 100 Red Cox Dr, St. Augustine, FL 32080

Description:

The St. Augustine Lighthouse and Maritime Museum offers stunning views of the Atlantic Ocean and a fascinating look at maritime history. This iconic lighthouse has been guiding ships since 1874.

Activities and Attractions:

Climb the 219 steps to the top for panoramic views, visit the museum to learn about shipwrecks and local history, and explore the grounds, which include a nature trail and playground.

Practical Information:

Open daily from 9:00 AM to 6:00 PM. Admission is $15.95 for adults and $13.95 for children. Discounts are available for military and seniors.

Local Tips:

Visit in the early morning or late afternoon to avoid peak crowds. Keep an eye out for ghost tours, as the lighthouse is rumored to be haunted!

Tallahassee Area

23. Wakulla Springs State Park

Location: Wakulla Springs, North Florida

Address: 465 Wakulla Park Dr, Wakulla Springs, FL 32327

Description:

Wakulla Springs State Park is home to one of the world's largest and deepest freshwater springs, surrounded by lush forests and teeming with wildlife. It's a serene escape for nature lovers.

Activities and Attractions:

Take a guided boat tour to see manatees, alligators, and birdlife. Enjoy swimming in the crystal-clear spring waters or explore the park's nature trails. The historic Wakulla Springs Lodge offers dining and overnight accommodations.

Practical Information:

The park is open daily from 8:00 AM to sunset. Admission is $6 per vehicle, and boat tours cost $8 for adults and $5 for children.

Local Tips:

Arrive early for the best chance of seeing manatees and other wildlife. Don't miss the park's diving platform for a refreshing plunge into the spring.

24. St. Marks Wildlife Refuge

Location: St. Marks, North Florida

Address: 1255 Lighthouse Rd, St. Marks, FL 32355

Description:

St. Marks Wildlife Refuge is a sprawling natural sanctuary known for its stunning landscapes, rich biodiversity, and the iconic St. Marks Lighthouse. It's a paradise for outdoor enthusiasts.

Activities and Attractions:

Explore the refuge's scenic trails, kayak through serene waterways, or enjoy birdwatching and wildlife photography. The lighthouse, dating back to 1831, is a highlight for history buffs.

Practical Information:

The refuge is open daily from sunrise to sunset. Entrance fees are $5 per vehicle. Annual passes are available for frequent visitors.

Local Tips:

Visit during the fall to witness the monarch butterfly migration. Bring binoculars and a camera to capture the area's abundant wildlife and breathtaking vistas.

25. Torreya State Park

Location: Bristol, North Florida

Address: 2576 NW Torreya Park Rd, Bristol, FL 32321

Description:

Torreya State Park is known for its dramatic landscapes, rare Torreya trees, and sweeping views of the Apalachicola River. It's a hiker's dream and a hidden gem in North Florida.

Activities and Attractions:

Hike the park's challenging trails, offering views of the river and unique geological features. Camping, picnicking, and birdwatching are popular activities. The historic Gregory House adds a touch of history to the park.

Practical Information:

The park is open daily from 8:00 AM to sunset. Admission is $3 per vehicle, and camping fees start at $16 per night.

Local Tips:

Hike the Torreya Challenge Trail for the best views, but be prepared for steep inclines. Fall is the ideal time to visit for cooler weather and vibrant foliage.

Florida Bucket List Destinations

CENTRAL FLORIDA

Crystal River

26. Crystal River (Swim with Manatees)

Location: Crystal River, Central Florida

Address: 1 SW 1st Pl, Crystal River, FL 34429

Description:

Crystal River is the only place in the United States where you can legally swim with manatees in their natural habitat. Known as the "Manatee Capital of the World," its crystal-clear waters provide an unforgettable wildlife experience.

Activities and Attractions:

Join a guided tour to snorkel alongside these gentle giants or observe them from a kayak. Explore nearby springs, like Three Sisters Springs, or take a scenic boat tour through Kings Bay.

Practical Information:

Tours operate year-round, but winter (November–March) is the best time, as manatees gather in the warm springs. Tour costs range from $50–$100 per person, and reservations are recommended.

Local Tips:

Book an early morning tour for fewer crowds and more manatee interactions. Wear a wetsuit to stay comfortable in the cool 72°F water, and bring an underwater camera for stunning close-up photos.

Lake Placid

27. Lake Placid Murals

Location: Lake Placid, Central Florida

Address: Downtown Lake Placid, FL 33852

Description:

Lake Placid, the "Town of Murals," boasts over 50 vibrant murals adorning its downtown buildings. These colorful works of art capture the town's history, culture, and natural beauty.

Activities and Attractions:

Take a self-guided walking tour to admire the murals and learn their stories. Stop by the Lake Placid Historical Society Depot Museum for a deeper dive into the town's heritage. Don't miss the quirky "Clown Museum," celebrating the town's connection to the circus.

Practical Information:

The murals are free to view and accessible year-round. Maps for the walking tour are available at the Chamber of Commerce. Parking is free throughout downtown.

Local Tips:

Visit early in the morning or late afternoon to avoid the midday heat. Bring a camera to capture the vibrant art and take a break at a local café for refreshments.

Merritt Island

28. Merritt Island Wildlife Refuge (Bioluminescence)

Location: Merritt Island, Central Florida

Address: 1987 Scrub Jay Way, Titusville, FL 32782

Description:

The Merritt Island Wildlife Refuge is a sprawling sanctuary teeming with wildlife, but its most magical feature is the bioluminescent waters. During the summer, microscopic organisms light up the waterways, creating a surreal experience.

Activities and Attractions:

Kayak through the glowing waters at night for an unforgettable bioluminescent tour. During the day, explore hiking trails, spot manatees and alligators, or enjoy birdwatching in this biodiverse haven.

Practical Information:

The refuge is open year-round, but bioluminescence tours are best from June to October. Entry is $10 per vehicle, and tour costs vary by provider, typically around $50–$75.

Local Tips:

Book a guided kayak tour for the best bioluminescent experience. Wear clothes you don't mind getting wet and bring insect repellent for evening visits.

Mount Dora

29. Mount Dora Downtown

Location: Mount Dora, Central Florida

Address: Downtown Mount Dora, FL 32757

Description:

Mount Dora's charming downtown is a treasure trove of boutique shops, art galleries, and quaint cafes. Known as the "Festival City," it's the perfect spot for a relaxed stroll and a taste of small-town charm.

Activities and Attractions:

Explore unique stores and antique shops, visit the Mount Dora History Museum, or enjoy al fresco dining with views of Lake Dora. Attend one of the town's famous festivals, such as the Mount Dora Arts Festival or the Christmas Lights Festival.

Practical Information:

The downtown area is free to explore and open year-round. Parking is available in public lots and on the street, with some areas charging a small fee during peak events.

Local Tips:

Visit during a festival for a lively experience or on weekdays for a quieter atmosphere. Stop by Donnelly Park for a picturesque photo opportunity.

Ocala

Wooden boardwalk in the recreation area in the Ocala National Forest located in Juniper Springs Florida

Shutterstock / Rafal Michal Gadomski

30. Mount Dora Scenic Boat Tours

Location: Mount Dora, Central Florida

Address: 100 N Alexander St, Mount Dora, FL 32757

Description:

The Mount Dora Scenic Boat Tours offer a relaxing way to explore the waterways of Lake Dora and the Dora Canal, often referred to as the "most beautiful mile of water in the world."

Activities and Attractions:

Cruise through lush cypress trees and spot wildlife, including herons, turtles, and even alligators. Learn about the area's history and ecosystem from knowledgeable guides.

Practical Information:

Tours operate daily, with tickets costing around $25 per adult and $15 per child. Reservations are recommended, especially during weekends and peak seasons.

Local Tips:

Bring a hat and sunscreen for daytime tours. For a romantic experience, book an evening cruise to catch the sunset over Lake Dora.

Ocala

31. Silver Springs State Park

Location: Ocala, Central Florida

Address: 5656 E Silver Springs Blvd, Silver Springs, FL 34488

Description:

Silver Springs State Park is famous for its crystal-clear waters and iconic glass-bottom boat tours. This natural wonder offers a glimpse into Florida's unique ecosystems and history.

Activities and Attractions:

Take a glass-bottom boat tour to see underwater springs and marine life. Enjoy kayaking, hiking, or picnicking in the park's serene surroundings. The Silver River Museum adds an educational element to your visit.

Practical Information:

The park is open daily from 8:00 AM to sunset. Admission is $8 per vehicle, and boat tours cost $13 per person.

Local Tips:

Visit early for a quieter experience and better wildlife viewing. Don't forget your camera to capture the stunning underwater views!

32. Juniper Springs Canoeing

Location: Ocala National Forest, Central Florida

Address: 26701 FL-40, Silver Springs, FL 34488

Description:

Juniper Springs is a picturesque spot for canoeing and kayaking, offering a serene journey through lush subtropical forests and crystal-clear waters.

Activities and Attractions:

Canoe or kayak along the seven-mile Juniper Run, one of Florida's most beautiful water trails. Enjoy swimming in the spring pool or exploring the historic millhouse.

Practical Information:

Open daily from 8:00 AM to 8:00 PM. Entry is $12 per vehicle, and canoe rentals start at $45. Reservations for rentals are recommended.

Local Tips:

Wear water shoes and bring plenty of sunscreen. Plan for 3–5 hours to complete the canoe run and pack snacks for the journey.

33. Rainbow Springs Tubing

Location: Dunnellon, Central Florida

Address: 10830 SW 180th Ave Rd, Dunnellon, FL 34432

Description:

Rainbow Springs is a tropical paradise known for its crystal-clear waters and lush surroundings. Tubing down the spring-fed Rainbow River is a relaxing and fun way to enjoy the scenery.

Activities and Attractions:

Rent a tube and float down the river, or explore hiking trails to see waterfalls and native plants. Snorkeling and swimming are also popular activities in the park.

Practical Information:

The tubing entrance is open seasonally, and rentals cost around $20 per person. Park entry is $2 per person.

Local Tips:

Arrive early, as tubing spots fill quickly. Bring a waterproof bag for your essentials and enjoy a leisurely float while soaking in the beauty.

34. Ocala National Forest

Location: Ocala, Central Florida

Address: 40929 State Road 19, Umatilla, FL 32784

Description:

Ocala National Forest is a sprawling natural area offering diverse ecosystems, from pine forests to sparkling springs. It's a haven for outdoor adventurers.

Activities and Attractions:

Hike or bike the many trails, swim or snorkel in springs like Alexander Springs, or enjoy camping under the stars. Fishing and boating are popular on the forest's lakes and rivers.

Practical Information:

The forest is open year-round, with no general admission fee. Some areas, like spring access points, have entry fees starting at $6 per person.

Local Tips:

Pack plenty of water and bug spray, especially during the warmer months. For a unique experience, explore the forest's off-the-beaten-path trails.

Orlando

35. Walt Disney World Resort

Location: Orlando, Central Florida

Address: 1375 E Buena Vista Dr, Orlando, FL 32830

Description:

The Walt Disney World Resort is a world-renowned destination offering four magical theme parks, two water parks, and endless entertainment. It's the ultimate family vacation spot.

Activities and Attractions:

Explore iconic parks like Magic Kingdom, EPCOT, Disney's Hollywood Studios, and Disney's Animal Kingdom. Enjoy thrilling rides, meet beloved characters, and experience dazzling parades and fireworks.

Practical Information:

Open daily with varying park hours. Ticket prices start at $109 per person per day, with discounts for multi-day passes. Reservations are required.

Local Tips:

Plan ahead with the My Disney Experience app for dining reservations and ride queues. Visit during weekdays for smaller crowds and cooler months for more comfortable weather.

36. Universal Studios Florida

Location: Orlando, Central Florida

Address: 6000 Universal Blvd, Orlando, FL 32819

Description:

Universal Studios Florida offers thrilling rides and immersive experiences based on blockbuster movies and TV shows. It's a must-visit for fans of action and adventure.

Activities and Attractions:

Ride attractions like Harry Potter and the Escape from Gringotts, meet characters, and explore themed areas such as Springfield and the Wizarding World of Harry Potter.

Practical Information:

Open daily with ticket prices starting at $109 per person. Express Passes are available for shorter wait times.

Local Tips:

Arrive early to avoid lines and stay late to enjoy nighttime shows. Don't miss trying Butterbeer at Diagon Alley!

37. LEGOLAND Florida Resort

Location: Winter Haven, Central Florida

Address: 1 LEGOLAND Way, Winter Haven, FL 33884

Description:

LEGOLAND Florida Resort is a theme park designed for families with younger children, featuring LEGO-themed rides, shows, and attractions.

Activities and Attractions:

Build and play in LEGO-inspired areas, ride family-friendly coasters, and explore the water park. The LEGO Movie World is a highlight for kids and adults alike.

Practical Information:

Open daily with ticket prices starting at $84 per person. Water park access requires an additional ticket.

Local Tips:

Visit midweek for smaller crowds and don't miss Miniland USA, featuring LEGO recreations of famous cities.

38. SeaWorld Orlando

Location: Orlando, Central Florida

Address: 7007 SeaWorld Dr, Orlando, FL 32821

Description:

SeaWorld Orlando is an aquatic theme park offering thrilling rides, marine animal encounters, and live shows.

Activities and Attractions:

Ride roller coasters like Mako, enjoy shows featuring dolphins and orcas, and visit interactive animal exhibits. Cool off at Aquatica, the adjacent water park.

Practical Information:

Open daily with ticket prices starting at $89.99. Discounts are available for multi-park passes.

Local Tips:

Check the schedule for showtimes and plan your day around them. Arrive early for animal feeding experiences.

39. Gatorland

Location: Orlando, Central Florida

Address: 14501 S Orange Blossom Trail, Orlando, FL 32837

Description:

Gatorland, known as the "Alligator Capital of the World," offers thrilling encounters with Florida's iconic reptiles in a family-friendly environment.

Activities and Attractions:

See thousands of alligators and crocodiles, enjoy live shows, and try the Screamin' Gator Zip Line for a bird's-eye view of the park.

Practical Information:

Open daily from 10:00 AM to 5:00 PM. Admission starts at $32.99 for adults and $22.99 for children.

Tampa

Beach front Tampa area Florida

Shutterstock / Joke van Eeghem

Local Tips:

Bring a camera for the unique photo ops, and don't miss the opportunity to hold a baby alligator!

40. Harry P. Leu Gardens

Location: Orlando, Central Florida

Address: 1920 N Forest Ave, Orlando, FL 32803

Description:

Harry P. Leu Gardens is a lush 50-acre botanical garden featuring stunning landscapes, scenic walking paths, and vibrant blooms throughout the year.

Activities and Attractions:

Explore themed gardens, including the butterfly garden and tropical stream garden. The historic Leu House Museum offers a glimpse into local history.

Practical Information:

Open daily from 9:00 AM to 5:00 PM. Admission is $15 for adults and $10 for children. Free entry is available on the first Monday of each month.

Local Tips:

Visit in spring to see the camellias and azaleas in full bloom. Bring a picnic and enjoy a relaxing day amidst nature.

Shark Valley (Everglades)

41. Shark Valley (Everglades Cycling and Tram Tours)

Location: Everglades National Park, South Florida

Address: 36000 SW 8th St, Miami, FL 33194

Description:

Shark Valley is a unique way to experience the Everglades, offering breathtaking views, abundant wildlife, and the famous 15-mile loop trail for cycling and tram tours.

Activities and Attractions:

Rent a bike or take a guided tram tour to explore the trail and spot alligators, herons, and turtles. Don't miss the observation tower, which offers panoramic views of the Everglades.

Practical Information:

Open daily from 8:30 AM to 6:00 PM. Entry to the park costs $30 per vehicle, with additional fees for bike rentals or tram tours.

Local Tips:

Visit early in the day to avoid heat and crowds. Pack sunscreen, water, and binoculars for wildlife spotting.

Tampa

42. Tampa Bay History Center

Location: Tampa, Central Florida

Address: 801 Water St, Tampa, FL 33602

Description:

The Tampa Bay History Center showcases 12,000 years of regional history, from indigenous cultures to modern-day Tampa. Interactive exhibits make it engaging for all ages.

Activities and Attractions:

Explore galleries on Florida's pirate history, cigar industry, and early settlers. Don't miss the Columbia Café for a taste of Tampa's culinary heritage.

Practical Information:

Open daily from 10:00 AM to 5:00 PM. Admission is $16.95 for adults and $12.95 for children. Discounts are available for seniors, students, and military.

Local Tips:

Plan to spend 2–3 hours exploring. Visit the Riverwalk afterward for scenic waterfront views.

43. Historic Ybor City

Location: Tampa, Central Florida

Address: 7th Avenue, Tampa, FL 33605

Description:

Ybor City, Tampa's historic Latin Quarter, is famous for its Cuban influence, vibrant nightlife, and rich cultural history. It's a National Historic Landmark District.

Activities and Attractions:

Take a walking tour to learn about the area's cigar-making history. Visit shops, galleries, and cafes, or enjoy the nightlife along 7th Avenue.

Practical Information:

Free to explore year-round. Some attractions, like the Ybor City Museum, charge admission. Parking is available in public lots and garages.

Local Tips:

Stop at Columbia Restaurant, a Tampa institution, for authentic Cuban cuisine. Visit during the annual Ybor City Cigar Heritage Festival.

Winter Park

44. Winter Park Scenic Boat Tour

Location: Winter Park, Central Florida

Address: 312 E Morse Blvd, Winter Park, FL 32789

Description:

The Winter Park Scenic Boat Tour takes you on a peaceful journey through the city's picturesque lakes and canals, surrounded by lush landscapes and historic homes.

Activities and Attractions:

Enjoy a guided boat ride with fascinating stories about Winter Park's history and landmarks. Spot wildlife, from herons to turtles, along the way.

Practical Information:

Tours operate daily from 10:00 AM to 4:00 PM. Tickets cost $16 for adults and $8 for children. Free parking is available nearby.

Local Tips:

Visit in the morning for calm waters and cooler temperatures. Combine your tour with a visit to the nearby Park Avenue for shopping and dining.

Lake Wales

45. Bok Tower Gardens

Location: Lake Wales, Central Florida

Address: 1151 Tower Blvd, Lake Wales, FL 33853

Description:

Bok Tower Gardens is a tranquil retreat featuring stunning gardens, serene walking paths, and the iconic 205-foot Singing Tower. It's a must-visit for nature lovers and art enthusiasts.

Activities and Attractions:

Stroll through the gardens, enjoy the soothing carillon music from the tower, and visit Pinewood Estate, a Mediterranean-style mansion.

Practical Information:

Open daily from 8:00 AM to 6:00 PM. Admission is $16 for adults and $5 for children. Free parking is available.

Local Tips:

Visit during spring for the most vibrant blooms. Bring a picnic to enjoy amidst the beautiful scenery.

Marianna

46. Florida Caverns State Park

Location: Marianna, North Florida

Address: 3345 Caverns Rd, Marianna, FL 32446

Description:

Florida Caverns State Park is the only state park in Florida offering guided tours of stunning limestone caves, featuring unique formations like stalactites and stalagmites.

Activities and Attractions:

Take a guided cave tour, hike nature trails, or enjoy kayaking and fishing along the Chipola River. The park also offers camping facilities.

Practical Information:

Open daily from 8:00 AM to sunset. Cave tours are $10 per adult and $5 per child, in addition to the $5 park entry fee.

Local Tips:

Wear comfortable shoes for the cave tour and bring a jacket, as the caves stay cool year-round. Arrive early, as tours often sell out.

Florida Bucket List Destinations

SOUTH FLORIDA

Anna Maria Island

47. Anna Maria Island Beaches

Location: Anna Maria Island, South Florida

Address: Anna Maria Island, FL 34216

Description:

Anna Maria Island Beaches offer a tranquil escape with powdery white sands, turquoise waters, and a charming old-Florida vibe. This barrier island is perfect for relaxation and reconnecting with nature.

Activities and Attractions:

Swim, sunbathe, or paddleboard in the calm Gulf waters. Explore the local shops and restaurants along Pine Avenue, or catch a stunning sunset at Bean Point.

Practical Information:

The beaches are free to access and open year-round. Parking is available but limited, so plan to arrive early.

Local Tips:

Bring your snorkeling gear to explore the shallow reefs. For a quieter experience, visit on a weekday and avoid peak holiday seasons.

Boca Grande

48. Gasparilla Island (Boca Grande)

Location: Boca Grande, South Florida

Address: Gasparilla Island, FL 33921

Description:

Gasparilla Island is known for its pristine beaches, historic charm, and the iconic Boca Grande Lighthouse. It's a peaceful destination ideal for beach lovers and history enthusiasts alike.

Activities and Attractions:

Relax on the beach, explore the Gasparilla Island State Park, or visit the historic lighthouse and museum. The island is also popular for fishing and shelling.

Practical Information:

Open year-round, with a $3 toll to access the island and a $3 entry fee for the state park. Parking is available near the beaches.

Local Tips:

Visit the lighthouse at sunset for incredible photo opportunities. Bike rentals are a great way to explore the island's scenic paths.

Boynton Beach

49. Boynton Beach Oceanfront Park

Location: Boynton Beach, South Florida

Address: 6415 N Ocean Blvd, Boynton Beach, FL 33435

Description:

Boynton Beach Oceanfront Park is a family-friendly destination with soft sands, lifeguard-protected waters, and picnic facilities. It's a favorite spot for a laid-back beach day.

Activities and Attractions:

Enjoy swimming, beachcombing, or relaxing in the shaded picnic areas. Kids will love the playground, while nature enthusiasts can explore the nearby dunes.

Practical Information:

The park is open daily from sunrise to sunset. Parking costs $10 per vehicle for non-residents.

Local Tips:

Arrive early to secure parking and a good spot on the beach. Don't miss the concession stand for snacks and cold drinks.

Clearwater

50. Clearwater Beach

Location: Clearwater, South Florida

Address: 1 Causeway Blvd, Clearwater, FL 33767

Description:

Clearwater Beach is a lively destination known for its soft white sands, vibrant atmosphere, and stunning Gulf views. It's consistently ranked among the best beaches in the U.S.

Activities and Attractions:

Swim, jet ski, or parasail in the clear waters. Visit Pier 60 for fishing, live entertainment, and breathtaking sunsets. The nearby marina offers dolphin-watching cruises.

Practical Information:

The beach is free to access, with parking available for a fee. The area is busiest during spring and summer.

Local Tips:

Visit early or during the offseason for fewer crowds. Check out the nightly Sunset Festival at Pier 60 for local crafts and performances.

Fort Myers

Majestic Great Blue Heron on the shore in Fort Myers Beach on the west coast of Florida

Shutterstock / Fotoluminate LLC

Coral Gables

51. Coral Gables Venetian Pool

Location: Coral Gables, South Florida

Address: 2701 De Soto Blvd, Coral Gables, FL 33134

Description:

The Venetian Pool is a historic, Mediterranean-style swimming pool filled with spring water. Surrounded by palm trees and waterfalls, it's a unique and refreshing destination.

Activities and Attractions:

Swim in the cool waters or relax in the shaded areas. Admire the pool's historic architecture and scenic landscaping.

Practical Information:

Open Tuesday through Sunday, with admission starting at $15 for non-residents. The pool is seasonal and closes during winter months.

Local Tips:

Arrive early, as the pool has a limited capacity. Check the schedule for family swim hours and pack a towel for lounging.

Fort Lauderdale

51. Fort Lauderdale's Las Olas Boulevard

Location: Fort Lauderdale, South Florida

Address: Las Olas Blvd, Fort Lauderdale, FL 33301

Description:

Las Olas Boulevard is Fort Lauderdale's premier destination for shopping, dining, and nightlife. This lively street offers a mix of culture, charm, and entertainment.

Activities and Attractions:

Browse boutique shops and art galleries, enjoy al fresco dining at world-class restaurants, or take a gondola tour along the canals. The nightlife here is vibrant and diverse.

Practical Information:

The boulevard is free to explore, with metered parking available along the street. Many restaurants and bars open late into the evening.

Local Tips:

Visit during the evening for a vibrant atmosphere. Don't miss the monthly art walks for unique local creations and live performances.

Fort Myers

52. Edison and Ford Winter Estates

Location: Fort Myers, South Florida

Address: 2350 McGregor Blvd, Fort Myers, FL 33901

Description:

The Edison and Ford Winter Estates offer a glimpse into the lives of two iconic inventors, Thomas Edison and Henry Ford. This historical site is a mix of innovation, history, and natural beauty.

Activities and Attractions:

Tour the historic homes, botanical gardens, and Edison's laboratory. Explore the museum, featuring artifacts, inventions, and vintage vehicles. Guided tours provide fascinating insights.

Practical Information:

Open daily from 9:00 AM to 5:30 PM. Admission starts at $25 for adults and $15 for children. Discounts are available for seniors and students.

Local Tips:

Visit during the holiday season for spectacular light displays. Don't miss the banyan tree, one of the largest in the U.S.

53. Fort Myers Beach

Location: Fort Myers, South Florida

Address: Estero Blvd, Fort Myers Beach, FL 33931

Description:

Fort Myers Beach is a lively destination with powdery white sands, calm Gulf waters, and a laid-back vibe. It's perfect for families, couples, and solo travelers.

Activities and Attractions:

Relax on the beach, swim, or try parasailing. Explore Times Square for shopping and dining, or take a dolphin-watching tour from the marina.

Practical Information:

Open year-round with free beach access. Parking is available for a fee at public lots.

Local Tips:

Arrive early to secure parking and enjoy a quieter morning. Stay for sunset, as the views are unforgettable.

Hollywood

54. Hollywood Beach Broadwalk

Location: Hollywood, South Florida

Address: 101 S Broadwalk, Hollywood, FL 33019

Description:

Hollywood Beach Broadwalk is a scenic, pedestrian-friendly stretch along the ocean. With shops, restaurants, and entertainment, it's ideal for a relaxing day by the beach.

Activities and Attractions:

Walk, bike, or rollerblade along the Broadwalk. Relax on the sandy beach, enjoy live music at the bandshell, or dine at waterfront restaurants.

Practical Information:

The Broadwalk is free to access and open year-round. Parking is available in nearby garages for a fee.

Local Tips:

Visit during the evening for a lively atmosphere and cooler weather. Don't miss the outdoor cinema events hosted seasonally.

Key Biscayne

55. Key Biscayne Lighthouse

Location: Key Biscayne, South Florida

Address: 1200 Crandon Blvd, Key Biscayne, FL 33149

Description:

The Key Biscayne Lighthouse, located in Bill Baggs Cape Florida State Park, is the oldest standing structure in Miami-Dade County. It's a historic gem with stunning ocean views.

Activities and Attractions:

Climb the lighthouse for panoramic views of the coastline. Explore the park's nature trails, picnic areas, and quiet beaches.

Practical Information:

The park is open daily, with a $5 entry fee per vehicle. Lighthouse tours are free and offered Thursday through Monday.

Local Tips:

Bring a picnic and enjoy the park's serene environment. Visit in the morning for cooler temperatures and fewer crowds.

Lover's Key

56. Lover's Key State Park

Location: Fort Myers Beach, South Florida

Address: 8700 Estero Blvd, Fort Myers Beach, FL 33931

Description:

Lover's Key State Park is a romantic getaway featuring pristine beaches, mangroves, and tranquil waterways. It's perfect for nature lovers and couples.

Activities and Attractions:

Kayak or paddleboard through mangrove trails, relax on the beach, or hike scenic nature trails. Wildlife spotting includes dolphins, manatees, and shorebirds.

Practical Information:

Open daily from 8:00 AM to sunset. Admission is $8 per vehicle. Kayak rentals are available on-site.

Local Tips:

Visit during low tide for better wildlife viewing. Pack a picnic and enjoy it at one of the park's shaded pavilions.

Marco Island

57. Marco Island Beaches

Location: Marco Island, South Florida

Address: Marco Island, FL 34145

Description:

Marco Island Beaches offer a luxurious escape with soft sands, sparkling waters, and a laid-back atmosphere. It's an ideal destination for relaxation and outdoor activities.

Activities and Attractions:

Swim, sunbathe, or go shelling along the shoreline. Take a boat tour to explore nearby Ten Thousand Islands or enjoy fine dining at waterfront restaurants.

Practical Information:

Beaches are free to access, but parking fees apply at public lots. Best visited in spring and fall for pleasant weather.

Local Tips:

Bring snorkeling gear for a chance to spot marine life near the shore. Sunset views from the beach are spectacular and not to be missed.

Matlacha (Pine Island)

58. Matlacha Art District

Location: Matlacha, South Florida

Address: Pine Island Rd NW, Matlacha, FL 33993

Description:

Matlacha Art District is a vibrant and quirky community known for its colorful buildings, art galleries, and unique charm. It's a haven for artists and creatives.

Activities and Attractions:

Browse galleries featuring local artwork, enjoy live music at waterfront bars, or shop for handmade crafts. The fishing pier is a favorite spot for relaxing.

Practical Information:

The district is free to explore and open year-round. Parking is available on the street and in small lots.

Local Tips:

Visit during the annual Pine Island Art Festival for a lively celebration of local creativity. Bring a camera to capture the vibrant murals and colorful facades.

Naples

Botanical garden with water feature pond decorative walkway with tropical palm trees and water lillies

Shutterstock / Gary G. Beeler

Miami

59. Art Deco Historic District

Location: Miami Beach, South Florida

Address: Ocean Drive, Miami Beach, FL 33139

Description:

The Art Deco Historic District in Miami Beach is famous for its vibrant, pastel-colored buildings and 1930s architecture. It's a unique blend of history and modern Miami flair.

Activities and Attractions:

Take a guided walking tour to learn about the district's history and architecture. Stroll along Ocean Drive to enjoy the iconic views, or dine in trendy sidewalk cafes.

Practical Information:

The district is free to explore, and guided tours are available for a fee. Parking is available in public lots and garages nearby.

Local Tips:

Visit in the evening to see the buildings lit up in neon lights. Don't miss the Art Deco Welcome Center for maps and additional information.

60. Miami Beach and South Beach

Location: Miami Beach, South Florida

Address: Miami Beach, FL 33139

Description:

Miami Beach and South Beach are iconic destinations known for their white sands, turquoise waters, and lively atmosphere. Perfect for sunbathing, water sports, and nightlife.

Activities and Attractions:

Relax on the beach, explore the shops and restaurants along Lincoln Road, or take a paddleboarding tour. The nightlife here is world-famous, with clubs and bars catering to all tastes.

Practical Information:

Free beach access is available year-round. Public parking lots are located nearby, with fees depending on the location and time of year.

Local Tips:

Visit early in the morning for quieter beaches and take a sunset walk along the shoreline for breathtaking views.

Naples

61. Naples Pier and Beaches

Location: Naples, South Florida

Address: 25 12th Ave S, Naples, FL 34102

Description:

Naples Pier is a historic landmark offering stunning Gulf views and a relaxed beach atmosphere. It's a favorite spot for fishing, strolling, and watching sunsets.

Activities and Attractions:

Walk the pier, enjoy sunbathing on the soft sands, or take a swim in the warm Gulf waters. Dolphins are frequently spotted near the pier.

Practical Information:

Open year-round with free access. Parking is available nearby for a fee.

Local Tips:

Visit at sunset for a magical view and bring binoculars for dolphin watching.

62. Naples Botanical Garden

Location: Naples, South Florida

Address: 4820 Bayshore Dr, Naples, FL 34112

Description:

Naples Botanical Garden is a 170-acre tropical paradise featuring themed gardens, walking trails, and vibrant blooms. It's a must-visit for nature enthusiasts and families.

Activities and Attractions:

Explore the themed gardens, including the Asian and Brazilian gardens, or take a peaceful walk around the butterfly house. Educational programs and art exhibits add to the experience.

Practical Information:

Open daily from 9:00 AM to 5:00 PM. Admission is $25 for adults and $10 for children. Free parking is available on-site.

Local Tips:

Visit in the morning to beat the heat and enjoy fewer crowds. Bring a picnic to enjoy in the serene surroundings.

Sarasota

63. The Ringling Museum of Art

Location: Sarasota, South Florida

Address: 5401 Bay Shore Rd, Sarasota, FL 34243

Description:

The Ringling Museum of Art is a cultural treasure featuring stunning galleries, a circus museum, and lush gardens. It's a mix of art, history, and entertainment.

Activities and Attractions:

Explore the art galleries, tour the Ca' d'Zan Mansion, and learn about circus history in the museum. Stroll through the rose garden and enjoy the waterfront views.

Practical Information:

Open daily from 10:00 AM to 5:00 PM. Admission is $25 for adults and $5 for children. Discounts are available for seniors and students.

Local Tips:

Visit on Mondays for free admission to the art museum. Allocate at least 3 hours to fully enjoy the site.

64. Sarasota Jungle Gardens

Location: Sarasota, South Florida

Address: 3701 Bay Shore Rd, Sarasota, FL 34234

Description:

Sarasota Jungle Gardens is a family-friendly attraction featuring lush tropical landscaping and interactive wildlife exhibits. It's perfect for kids and nature lovers.

Activities and Attractions:

Hand-feed flamingos, watch wildlife shows, and explore walking paths surrounded by exotic plants. The petting zoo is a hit with younger visitors.

Practical Information:

Open daily from 10:00 AM to 5:00 PM. Admission is $19.99 for adults and $12.99 for children. Parking is free.

Local Tips:

Bring sunscreen and water for your visit. Plan to attend the interactive animal shows for a fun and educational experience.

65. Siesta Key Beach

Location: Siesta Key, Sarasota, South Florida

Address: 948 Beach Rd, Sarasota, FL 34242

Description:

Siesta Key Beach is consistently ranked among the best beaches in the world, with powdery white quartz sand and clear turquoise waters.

Activities and Attractions:

Enjoy swimming, sunbathing, or playing volleyball on the beach. The nearby village offers charming shops and restaurants.

Practical Information:

Free beach access and parking are available year-round. Lifeguards are on duty during daylight hours.

Local Tips:

Arrive early to secure parking, especially on weekends. Stay for sunset to experience Siesta Key's famous evening skies.

Solomon's Castle (Ona)

66. Solomon's Castle

Location: Ona, South Florida

Address: 4533 Solomon Rd, Ona, FL 33865

Description:

Solomon's Castle is an eccentric masterpiece created by artist Howard Solomon. This shiny, castle-like structure is made from recycled materials and houses unique art pieces.

Activities and Attractions:

Take a guided tour of the castle, explore the art gallery, and enjoy lunch at the on-site Boat-in-the-Moat restaurant.

Practical Information:

Open Tuesday through Sunday, with tours costing $10 per person. Parking is free.

Local Tips:

Bring a camera to capture the quirky architecture. Plan to stay for lunch, as the restaurant offers delicious and unique dishes.

Venice

67. Venice Beach (Shark Tooth Capital)

Location: Venice, South Florida

Address: 101 The Esplanade, Venice, FL 34285

Description:

Venice Beach is famous for its soft sands and as the "Shark Tooth Capital of the World." It's a must-visit for beachcombers and fossil hunters.

Activities and Attractions:

Search for fossilized shark teeth along the shoreline, swim in the warm Gulf waters, or relax under the Florida sun.

Practical Information:

The beach is free to access, with parking available nearby. Open year-round.

Local Tips:

Bring a sifting tool for shark tooth hunting and arrive early to avoid crowds.

Everglades Region

68. Everglades National Park

Location: Homestead, South Florida

Address: 40001 State Hwy 9336, Homestead, FL 33034

Description:

Everglades National Park is a UNESCO World Heritage Site, showcasing one of the world's most unique ecosystems. This subtropical wilderness is home to diverse wildlife, including alligators, manatees, and rare birds.

Activities and Attractions:

Explore the park's trails, kayak through mangroves, or take a guided airboat tour. Popular spots include Anhinga Trail for wildlife viewing and Flamingo Visitor Center for water activities.

Practical Information:

The park is open daily. Entrance fees are $30 per vehicle or $15 per person. Boat and kayak rentals are available at select visitor centers.

Local Tips:

Visit early morning or late afternoon for the best wildlife activity. Bring insect repellent and wear comfortable walking shoes.

69. Big Cypress National Preserve

Location: Ochopee, South Florida

Address: 33100 Tamiami Trail E, Ochopee, FL 34141

Description:

Big Cypress National Preserve features vast wetlands and cypress forests, providing a crucial habitat for Florida panthers, alligators, and diverse bird species.

Activities and Attractions:

Hike scenic trails, kayak through tranquil waterways, or take a swamp buggy tour for a closer look at the preserve's unique environment.

Practical Information:

Open year-round with no entrance fees. Ranger-led programs are available seasonally.

Local Tips:

Visit in the cooler winter months to avoid mosquitoes and high temperatures. Stop at the Oasis Visitor Center for wildlife viewing and trail information.

70. Shark Valley (Everglades Cycling and Tram Tours)

Location: Everglades National Park, South Florida

Address: 36000 SW 8th St, Miami, FL 33194

Description:

Shark Valley offers an immersive experience in the Everglades with a 15-mile paved loop trail ideal for cycling and tram tours. The observation tower provides breathtaking views of the wetlands.

Activities and Attractions:

Rent a bike or join a tram tour to explore the trail, spotting alligators and birds along the way. The observation tower is a highlight for panoramic views.

Practical Information:

Open daily from 8:30 AM to 6:00 PM. Entrance fees are $30 per vehicle. Bike rentals and tram tours are additional.

Local Tips:

Visit early to avoid heat and crowds. Bring sunscreen, water, and binoculars for wildlife viewing.

Jupiter Area

71. Blowing Rocks Preserve

Location: Hobe Sound, South Florida

Address: 574 S Beach Rd, Hobe Sound, FL 33455

Description:

Blowing Rocks Preserve is a unique coastal habitat featuring limestone formations that create dramatic water sprays during high tide. It's a serene spot for nature lovers.

Activities and Attractions:

Walk along the beach to see the striking rock formations, explore trails through native vegetation, and visit the preserve's educational center.

Practical Information:

Open daily from 9:00 AM to 4:30 PM. Admission is $2 per person. Parking is limited, so plan to arrive early.

Local Tips:

Visit during high tide for the most spectacular water sprays. Bring sturdy shoes for walking along the rocky shore.

Caladesi Island

72. Caladesi Island State Park

Location: Dunedin, Central Florida

Address: Accessible by ferry from Honeymoon Island, Dunedin, FL 34698

Description:

Caladesi Island State Park is a secluded paradise known for its pristine beaches, crystal-clear waters, and lush coastal hammocks. It's perfect for a relaxing day trip.

Activities and Attractions:

Swim, sunbathe, or paddleboard along the Gulf's calm waters. Explore nature trails or kayak through mangrove tunnels for a peaceful adventure.

Practical Information:

Accessible by ferry, which costs $16 per adult and $8 per child. The park is open daily, and parking is available at Honeymoon Island for $8 per vehicle.

Local Tips:

Pack snacks and drinks, as amenities are limited. Visit during the morning for cooler weather and fewer crowds.

Florida Bucket List Destinations

FLORIDA KEYS

Big Pine Key

73. Big Pine Key (Key Deer Refuge)

Location: Big Pine Key, South Florida

Address: 179 Key Deer Blvd, Big Pine Key, FL 33043

Description:

The National Key Deer Refuge is a protected habitat for the endangered Key deer, a small and charming species unique to the Florida Keys. It's a peaceful destination for wildlife enthusiasts.

Activities and Attractions:

Explore hiking trails through pine rocklands, mangroves, and wetlands. Stop by the visitor center to learn about conservation efforts and the local ecosystem. Wildlife viewing, especially of Key deer, is a highlight.

Practical Information:

Open daily from sunrise to sunset, with free entry. The visitor center is open Monday through Saturday with no admission fee.

Local Tips:

Visit early morning or evening for the best chance to spot Key deer. Drive carefully in the area to protect these endangered animals.

74. Shark Tooth Hunting in the Keys

Location: Various beaches in the Keys

Address: Accessible locations include Bahia Honda State Park and Sombrero Beach.

Description:

The Florida Keys are a hidden gem for finding fossilized shark teeth, a favorite activity for collectors and beachcombers.

Activities and Attractions:

Search for shark teeth along the shores, particularly after storms or during low tide. Combine your hunting with a relaxing day at the beach.

Practical Information:

Beach access is typically free or included in state park admission fees. The best time to hunt is after storms when fresh finds wash ashore.

Local Tips:

Bring a small sieve or mesh bag to sift through sand and shallow waters. Early mornings and low tide offer the best opportunities.

Cudjoe Key

74. Cudjoe Key Wildlife Refuge

Location: Cudjoe Key, South Florida

Address: Accessible via US-1, Cudjoe Key, FL 33042

Description:

Cudjoe Key Wildlife Refuge is part of the Florida Keys National Wildlife Refuges and offers a quiet retreat for nature enthusiasts. Its mangroves and wetlands support diverse wildlife.

Activities and Attractions:

Kayak or paddleboard through mangrove-lined waterways, hike scenic trails, or birdwatch for rare species like the white-crowned pigeon.

Practical Information:

Open year-round with no entry fee. Kayak rentals are available at nearby outfitters.

Local Tips:

Visit at sunrise for serene paddling and optimal wildlife activity. Bring binoculars for spotting birds and other wildlife.

Dry Tortugas

75. Dry Tortugas National Park

Location: 70 miles west of Key West, South Florida

Address: Accessible only by ferry or seaplane from Key West.

Description:

Dry Tortugas National Park is a remote oasis featuring turquoise waters, coral reefs, and historic Fort Jefferson. It's one of Florida's most unique and stunning destinations.

Activities and Attractions:

Snorkel among vibrant coral reefs, tour the historic fort, or relax on pristine sandy beaches. Birdwatching and kayaking are also popular activities.

Practical Information:

Open year-round. Ferry tickets cost approximately $200 per person, including park entry. Camping is available for $15 per night, but reservations are essential.

Local Tips:

Bring plenty of water, sunscreen, and snacks, as amenities are limited. Stay overnight to enjoy stargazing in this remote paradise.

Islamorada

76. Islamorada (Sportfishing Capital)

Location: Islamorada, South Florida

Address: Islamorada, FL 33036

Description:

Known as the "Sportfishing Capital of the World," Islamorada offers unparalleled fishing opportunities, attracting anglers from around the globe. Its waters are teeming with game fish like tarpon, sailfish, and bonefish.

Activities and Attractions:

Charter a fishing boat for a guided trip or try your luck from the shore. For a unique experience, visit the History of Diving Museum to learn about the area's marine heritage.

Key Largo

Molasses Reef in Key Largo Florida with Grunts and Sponges

Shutterstock / Kristen Lopez

Practical Information:

Fishing charters vary in price, starting around $400 for a half-day trip. Peak fishing seasons depend on the species, so check ahead for the best timing.

Local Tips:

Book charters in advance, especially during peak seasons. Bring a hat, sunscreen, and your camera to capture your catch of the day.

77. Robbie's Marina (Feed the Tarpon)

Location: Islamorada, South Florida

Address: 77522 Overseas Hwy, Islamorada, FL 33036

Description:

Robbie's Marina is a must-visit destination where you can hand-feed massive tarpon, a thrilling and memorable experience for all ages.

Activities and Attractions:

Feed the tarpon, rent a kayak for a paddle through nearby mangroves, or browse local art and souvenirs at the marina's shops.

Practical Information:

Open daily from 7:00 AM to 6:00 PM. Feeding costs $2.50 per person plus $5 for a bucket of fish.

Local Tips:

Arrive early to avoid crowds and bring cash for the tarpon feeding. Watch for pelicans—they love to steal the bait!

78. Kayaking Through Mangroves

Location: Islamorada, South Florida

Address: Various launch points, including Robbie's Marina and Indian Key Historic State Park

Description:

Kayaking through Islamorada's mangrove tunnels offers a peaceful and scenic adventure. It's an excellent way to explore the area's unique ecosystem up close.

Activities and Attractions:

Paddle through serene waterways, spot wildlife like herons and manatees, and enjoy the natural beauty of Florida's coastal mangroves.

Practical Information:

Kayak rentals start at $40 for a half-day. Guided tours are also available for those seeking a more informative experience.

Local Tips:

Bring water shoes and sunscreen, and choose a guided tour for the best routes and wildlife insights. Early morning trips offer cooler weather and calmer waters.

79. Snorkeling the Florida Keys Wreck Trail

Location: Islamorada, South Florida

Address: Accessible by boat, Islamorada, FL 33036

Description:

The Florida Keys Wreck Trail features a series of shipwrecks teeming with marine life. Islamorada offers some of the best snorkeling and diving spots along this underwater treasure trove.

Activities and Attractions:

Snorkel or dive to explore shipwrecks like the Eagle, a freighter covered in coral and home to vibrant fish species. Guided tours provide gear and expert knowledge.

Practical Information:

Charter boats and tours are available, with costs starting at $75 per person. Gear rental is often included.

Local Tips:

Check weather conditions before booking, as visibility is best on calm days. Bring an underwater camera to capture the stunning marine life.

John Pennekamp Coral Reef State Park (Key Largo)

80. John Pennekamp Coral Reef State Park

Location: Key Largo, South Florida

Address: 102601 Overseas Hwy, Key Largo, FL 33037

Description:

John Pennekamp Coral Reef State Park is the first undersea park in the U.S., protecting vibrant coral reefs and abundant marine life. It's a top destination for snorkeling and scuba diving.

Activities and Attractions:

Snorkel or dive among coral reefs, explore mangrove trails by kayak, or take a glass-bottom boat tour. The visitor center features aquariums and educational exhibits.

Practical Information:

Open daily from 8:00 AM to sunset. Admission is $8 per vehicle, and snorkeling tours start at $38 per person.

Local Tips:

Book snorkeling tours in advance and bring reef-safe sunscreen. Early morning trips often provide the calmest waters and best visibility.

Key Largo

81. Key Largo Coral Reef State Park

Location: Key Largo, South Florida

Address: 102601 Overseas Hwy, Key Largo, FL 33037

Description:

Key Largo Coral Reef State Park, part of John Pennekamp Coral Reef State Park, offers breathtaking underwater ecosystems and vibrant coral reefs. It's a paradise for snorkelers and divers.

Activities and Attractions:

Snorkel or dive among colorful reefs, enjoy kayaking through mangrove trails, or take a glass-bottom boat tour for a unique perspective. Visit the visitor center for educational exhibits and aquariums.

Practical Information:

Open daily from 8:00 AM to sunset. Park admission is $8 per vehicle, and snorkeling tours start at $38 per person.

Local Tips:

Bring reef-safe sunscreen and a waterproof camera. Morning tours often provide the calmest waters and best visibility.

82. Kayaking Through Mangroves

Location: Key Largo, South Florida

Address: Launch points include John Pennekamp Coral Reef State Park

Description:

Kayaking through Key Largo's mangrove trails offers a serene adventure through a rich and biodiverse environment. These winding waterways are perfect for spotting wildlife.

Activities and Attractions:

Paddle through mangrove tunnels, observe birds, fish, and crabs, and immerse yourself in the natural beauty of the Keys.

Practical Information:

Kayak rentals start at $40 for a half-day. Guided tours are available for additional fees.

Local Tips:

Wear water shoes and insect repellent. Early morning paddles are ideal for cooler temperatures and more active wildlife.

83. Snorkeling the Florida Keys Wreck Trail

Location: Key Largo, South Florida

Address: Accessible by boat from various locations

Description:

The Florida Keys Wreck Trail is a series of shipwrecks transformed into thriving marine habitats. Key Largo is home to some of the most famous wrecks, perfect for snorkelers and divers.

Activities and Attractions:

Explore shipwrecks like the Spiegel Grove and Benwood Wreck, home to vibrant coral and fish species. Guided tours provide safe and informative access to these underwater treasures.

Practical Information:

Snorkeling tours start at $75 per person, with gear rental often included. Advanced certification may be required for some dives.

Local Tips:

Book tours on calm days for the best visibility. Bring an underwater camera to capture the stunning marine life and shipwrecks.

84. Shark Tooth Hunting in the Keys

Location: Beaches around Key Largo and surrounding Keys

Address: Key Largo beaches and state parks

Description:

Key Largo is a hidden gem for fossilized shark tooth hunting. With a little patience and the right tools, you can uncover these ancient treasures along the shore.

Activities and Attractions:

Comb beaches for shark teeth, especially after storms. Combine this relaxing activity with a day of sunbathing or swimming.

Practical Information:

Beach access is free at most locations, or included with park entry fees. Best times for hunting are early morning or after storms.

Local Tips:

Bring a sieve or small shovel to sift through sand and shallow water. Wear water shoes for comfort while searching along rocky areas.

Key West

85. Key West and Mallory Square

Location: Key West, South Florida

Address: Mallory Square, Key West, FL 33040

Description:

Key West is a vibrant island filled with colorful architecture, lively culture, and iconic sunsets. Mallory Square is the heart of Key West, known for its nightly Sunset Celebration.

Activities and Attractions:

Stroll Duval Street for shops, galleries, and restaurants. At Mallory Square, enjoy live music, street performers, and local crafts as the sun sets over the Gulf.

Practical Information:

Mallory Square is free to visit. Sunset Celebration starts about an hour before sunset. Parking is available nearby for a fee.

Local Tips:

Arrive early for the best viewing spots and bring cash for local vendors.

86. Ernest Hemingway House

Location: Key West, South Florida

Address: 907 Whitehead St, Key West, FL 33040

Description:

The Ernest Hemingway House offers a glimpse into the life of one of America's greatest authors. This charming home is famous for its six-toed cats and literary history.

Activities and Attractions:

Tour the house and gardens, learn about Hemingway's life, and meet the descendants of his six-toed cats.

Practical Information:

Open daily from 9:00 AM to 5:00 PM. Admission is $17 for adults and $7 for children.

Key West

Key West famous Duval street view, south Florida Keys, United states of America

Shutterstock / xbrchx

Local Tips:

Visit early to avoid crowds and enjoy a peaceful tour of the lush gardens.

87. Fort Zachary Taylor Historic State Park

Location: Key West, South Florida

Address: 601 Howard England Way, Key West, FL 33040

Description:

Fort Zachary Taylor combines history and natural beauty, featuring a Civil War-era fort and one of the best beaches in Key West.

Activities and Attractions:

Tour the historic fort, relax on the beach, or snorkel in the clear waters. Hiking and biking trails offer scenic views of the surrounding area.

Practical Information:

Open daily from 8:00 AM to sunset. Admission is $6 per vehicle.

Local Tips:

Bring water shoes for snorkeling and enjoy a picnic under the shaded pavilions.

Little Torch Key

88. Little Torch Key (Secluded Escape)

Location: Little Torch Key, South Florida

Address: Little Torch Key, FL 33042

Description:

Little Torch Key is a serene getaway, known for its tranquil ambiance and luxurious resorts. It's perfect for a romantic or peaceful escape.

Activities and Attractions:

Enjoy private beaches, kayaking, and fishing. Explore the nearby islands by boat or simply relax in the quiet atmosphere.

Practical Information:

Open year-round. Accommodations range from boutique inns to luxury resorts.

Local Tips:

Stay at Little Palm Island Resort for an exclusive experience. Book activities in advance to make the most of your stay.

Long Key

89. Long Key State Park

Location: Long Key, South Florida

Address: 67400 Overseas Hwy, Long Key, FL 33001

Description:

Long Key State Park is a natural retreat offering stunning views, tranquil waters, and opportunities for outdoor adventures.

Activities and Attractions:

Kayak through mangroves, hike scenic trails, or enjoy fishing along the shore. The shallow waters are perfect for snorkeling.

Practical Information:

Open daily from 8:00 AM to sunset. Admission is $5 per vehicle.

Local Tips:

Visit during low tide for the best wildlife viewing along the shoreline.

Marathon

90. Marathon's Turtle Hospital

Location: Marathon, South Florida

Address: 2396 Overseas Hwy, Marathon, FL 33050

Description:

The Turtle Hospital is a rescue and rehabilitation center dedicated to saving sea turtles. Visitors can learn about conservation efforts and meet rescued turtles.

Activities and Attractions:

Take a guided tour, view the rehabilitation tanks, and see turtles up close. Educational programs provide insights into marine life.

Practical Information:

Open daily. Tours cost $30 for adults and $15 for children.

Local Tips:

Book tours in advance, as spots fill quickly. Bring a camera to capture your experience.

91. Bioluminescent Kayaking

Location: Marathon, South Florida

Address: Launch points vary; check with local tour operators

Description:

Kayaking in bioluminescent waters is a magical experience where microorganisms light up the water with a glowing blue-green hue.

Activities and Attractions:

Paddle through glowing waters and watch as your movements create a shimmering effect. Tours often include insights into the phenomenon.

Practical Information:

Best experienced in summer. Tours cost around $50 per person.

Local Tips:

Choose a moonless night for the brightest bioluminescence. Wear quick-drying clothes and bring water shoes.

92. Kayaking Through Mangroves

Location: Marathon, South Florida

Address: Various launch points, including Curry Hammock State Park

Description:

Explore Marathon's peaceful mangrove tunnels by kayak, where you'll encounter diverse wildlife and stunning natural scenery.

Activities and Attractions:

Paddle through mangroves, spot birds and marine life, and enjoy the tranquility of the Keys' unique ecosystem.

Practical Information:

Kayak rentals start at $40 for a half-day. Guided tours are available for an additional fee.

Local Tips:

Visit early morning for cooler weather and more active wildlife.

Sugarloaf Key

93. Sugarloaf Key Bat Tower

Location: Sugarloaf Key, South Florida

Address: Bat Tower Rd, Sugarloaf Key, FL 33042

Description:

The Sugarloaf Key Bat Tower is a quirky historical landmark built in 1929 to control mosquito populations. Though bats never took residence, it remains a fascinating roadside attraction.

Activities and Attractions:

Explore the site and learn about its history and unique construction. It's a great stop for photos and a bit of local lore.

Practical Information:

Open year-round and free to visit.

Local Tips:

Combine your visit with a trip to nearby wildlife refuges for a full day of exploration.

Part 2

Hidden Gems Deep Dive

NATURAL PARADISES

Chiefland

94. Manatee Springs State Park

Location: Chiefland, North Florida

Address: 11650 NW 115th St, Chiefland, FL 32626

Description:

Manatee Springs State Park is a lush natural oasis where crystal-clear waters bubble from underground springs, creating a perfect habitat for manatees in winter months.

Activities and Attractions:

Swim, kayak, or snorkel in the spring's refreshing waters. Hike scenic boardwalk trails through the cypress forest, and enjoy wildlife spotting, including manatees and turtles.

Practical Information:

Open daily from 8:00 AM to sunset. Admission is $6 per vehicle. Kayak rentals are available on-site.

Local Tips:

Visit in winter for the best chance to see manatees. Bring a picnic to enjoy under the park's shaded pavilions.

Copeland

95. Fakahatchee Strand Preserve State Park

Location: Copeland, South Florida

Address: 137 Coastline Dr, Copeland, FL 34137

Description:

Known as the "Amazon of North America," Fakahatchee Strand Preserve is a biodiversity hotspot featuring orchids, bromeliads, and unique wildlife like the elusive Florida panther.

Activities and Attractions:

Hike or bike through scenic trails, kayak through swampy waterways, and look for rare orchids. The Big Cypress Bend Boardwalk offers a family-friendly introduction to the park.

Practical Information:

Open daily from 8:00 AM to sunset. Admission is $3 per vehicle. Guided tours are available seasonally.

Local Tips:

Visit in winter or spring for cooler weather and fewer bugs. Wear waterproof shoes for exploring the wet trails.

Gainesville

96. Devil's Millhopper Geological State Park

Location: Gainesville, North Florida

Address: 4732 Millhopper Rd, Gainesville, FL 32653

Description:

This unique park features a massive sinkhole that plunges 120 feet into a miniature rainforest ecosystem, offering a glimpse into Florida's geological past.

Activities and Attractions:

Descend the wooden staircase to the bottom of the sinkhole, enjoying the lush vegetation and cascading waterfalls along the way.

Practical Information:

Open Wednesday through Sunday from 9:00 AM to 5:00 PM. Admission is $4 per vehicle.

Local Tips:

Visit after rain to see the waterfalls at their fullest. Wear comfortable shoes for navigating the stairs.

Islamorada

97. Windley Key Fossil Reef Geological State Park

Location: Islamorada, South Florida

Address: 84900 Overseas Hwy, Islamorada, FL 33036

Description:

This park is a geological wonder, showcasing fossilized coral reefs that were quarried for building the Overseas Highway in the early 20th century.

Activities and Attractions:

Take a self-guided tour of the fossilized coral formations and learn about the site's history and geology. Hiking trails offer a serene escape into native vegetation.

Practical Information:

Open Thursday through Monday from 8:00 AM to 5:00 PM. Admission is $2.50 per person.

Local Tips:

Bring a magnifying glass to better examine the fossilized coral details.

Jupiter

98. Blowing Rocks Preserve

Location: Hobe Sound, South Florida

Address: 574 S Beach Rd, Hobe Sound, FL 33455

Description:

Blowing Rocks Preserve features dramatic limestone formations that create impressive water sprays during high tide, a rare sight in Florida.

Activities and Attractions:

Walk along the beach to admire the unique rock formations, explore the preserve's trails, and visit the education center to learn about conservation efforts.

Practical Information:

Open daily from 9:00 AM to 4:30 PM. Admission is $2 per person.

Local Tips:

Visit during high tide for the most dramatic sprays. Wear sturdy shoes for navigating the rocky shoreline.

Ocala National Forest

The recreation area in the Ocala National Forest located in Juniper Springs Florida, USA

Shutterstock / Rafal Michal Gadomski

Live Oak

99. Peacock Springs State Park

Location: Live Oak, North Florida

Address: 12087 SW US Hwy 27, Mayo, FL 32066

Description:

Peacock Springs State Park is a haven for cave divers, featuring two major springs and miles of underwater caves. It's also a peaceful retreat for nature lovers.

Activities and Attractions:

Cave dive in the park's crystal-clear waters, swim in the springs, or hike the scenic trails. Educational signs provide insights into the park's ecosystem.

Practical Information:

Open daily from 8:00 AM to sunset. Admission is $4 per vehicle.

Local Tips:

Bring snorkeling gear to explore the spring areas. Diving requires proper certification.

Ocala National Forest

100. Juniper Prairie Wilderness

Location: Silver Springs, Central Florida

Address: Accessible via Juniper Springs Recreation Area

Description:

This pristine wilderness area in Ocala National Forest offers stunning landscapes of prairies, hammocks, and clear waterways.

Activities and Attractions:

Hike the Florida Trail, kayak the crystal-clear Juniper Run, or enjoy birdwatching in the serene environment.

Practical Information:

Open year-round with an entry fee of $8 per vehicle at Juniper Springs Recreation Area.

Local Tips:

Pack plenty of water and wear sturdy shoes for hiking. Visit in spring or fall for cooler weather.

St. Petersburg

101. Egmont Key State Park

Location: Egmont Key, South Florida

Address: Accessible only by ferry or private boat

Description:

Egmont Key State Park is a secluded island featuring historical ruins, a working lighthouse, and pristine beaches.

Activities and Attractions:

Explore historic sites, snorkel in clear waters, and relax on sandy beaches. The island is also a haven for birdwatchers.

Practical Information:

Open daily from 8:00 AM to sunset. Ferry tickets start at $25 per person.

Local Tips:

Bring sunscreen, water, and snacks, as there are no amenities on the island.

White Springs

102. Big Shoals State Park

Location: White Springs, North Florida

Address: 11330 SE Co Rd 135, White Springs, FL 32096

Description:

Big Shoals State Park is home to Florida's largest whitewater rapids, offering a unique and thrilling natural experience.

Activities and Attractions:

Hike or bike trails with views of the Suwannee River and the rapids. Picnic areas provide a perfect spot to relax after exploring.

Practical Information:

Open daily from 8:00 AM to sunset. Admission is $4 per vehicle.

Local Tips:

Visit after heavy rains for the most impressive rapids. Wear sturdy shoes for hiking.

Dog Island (Gulf Coast)

103. Dog Island

Location: Dog Island, Gulf Coast, North Florida

Address: Accessible by boat or private ferry from Carrabelle, FL 32322

Description:

Dog Island is a secluded paradise known for its unspoiled beaches, crystal-clear waters, and abundant wildlife. It's a tranquil escape for those seeking peace and natural beauty.

Activities and Attractions:

Relax on pristine beaches, kayak along the shoreline, or explore hiking trails that wind through pine forests and dunes. Birdwatching is excellent, with various migratory species passing through.

Practical Information:

Open year-round. Access is via private boat or ferry. The island is mostly undeveloped, so bring all necessities, including food and water.

Local Tips:

Visit during the week for even more solitude. Pack binoculars for wildlife spotting and sunscreen for long beach days.

Blue Spring (Orange City)

104. Blue Spring State Park

Location: Orange City, Central Florida

Address: 2100 W French Ave, Orange City, FL 32763

Description:

Blue Spring State Park is a winter haven for manatees, featuring crystal-clear waters and a lush, natural setting. It's perfect for swimming, hiking, and wildlife viewing.

Activities and Attractions:

Swim, snorkel, or kayak in the spring run during the warmer months. In winter, observe manatees from boardwalks. Hiking trails provide scenic views of the St. Johns River.

Practical Information:

Open daily from 8:00 AM to sunset. Admission is $6 per vehicle. Swimming is closed during manatee season (mid-November to March).

Local Tips:

Arrive early as the park reaches capacity quickly. Visit in winter for manatee spotting or spring for water activities.

Devil's Den (Williston)

105. Devil's Den Prehistoric Spring

Location: Williston, North Florida

Address: 5390 NE 180th Ave, Williston, FL 32696

Description:

Devil's Den is a unique, prehistoric underground spring featuring crystal-clear waters and a dramatic karst cave setting. It's a must-visit for snorkeling and diving enthusiasts.

Activities and Attractions:

Snorkel or scuba dive to explore the spring's underwater formations. Above ground, enjoy picnicking or relaxing in the serene surroundings.

Practical Information:

Open daily, but reservations are required for all activities. Snorkeling costs $25 per person. Guests must be at least 18 years old or accompanied by an adult.

Local Tips:

Visit early for smaller crowds. Bring a wetsuit, as the water remains a cool 72°F year-round.

St. Vincent Island (Apalachicola)

106. St. Vincent Island

Location: Apalachicola, North Florida

Address: Accessible by boat from Indian Pass, FL

Description:

St. Vincent Island is a remote wildlife refuge featuring pristine beaches, salt marshes, and diverse habitats. It's an ideal destination for nature lovers and adventurers.

Activities and Attractions:

Explore hiking and biking trails, enjoy fishing or kayaking, and observe wildlife, including red wolves and migratory birds.

Practical Information:

Open year-round and free to visit. Access is by private boat or shuttle service from Indian Pass.

Local Tips:

Bring plenty of water and supplies, as there are no amenities on the island. Visit during cooler months for more comfortable hiking conditions.

Cayo Costa (Pine Island Sound)

107. Cayo Costa State Park

Location: Pine Island Sound, South Florida

Address: Accessible by ferry from Pine Island or Captiva Island

Description:

Cayo Costa State Park is a remote barrier island offering white sand beaches, turquoise waters, and untouched natural beauty.

Activities and Attractions:

Swim, snorkel, or kayak in the clear waters. Hike or bike through nature trails, or enjoy shelling along the beach. Primitive camping is available for overnight stays.

Practical Information:

Open daily from 8:00 AM to sunset. Ferry tickets start at $40 per person. Camping fees are $22 per night.

Local Tips:

Pack food, water, and sunscreen, as there are no stores on the island. Stay overnight for stunning sunsets and stargazing.

Apalachicola

Dusk sky over Apalachicola bay on the Carrabelle beach

Shutterstock / Fomo Photography

Hidden Gems Deep Dive

CULTURAL AND HISTORIC SITES

Cedar Key

108. Cedar Key Museum State Park

Location: Cedar Key, North Florida

Address: 12231 SW 166th Ct, Cedar Key, FL 32625

Description:

Cedar Key Museum State Park offers a glimpse into the island's rich history and natural beauty. The museum showcases artifacts from Cedar Key's fishing and timber industries and the home of 19th-century naturalist St. Clair Whitman.

Activities and Attractions:

Explore the museum exhibits, stroll through the park's scenic trails, and enjoy views of the surrounding waters. Birdwatching is popular, with many coastal species frequenting the area.

Practical Information:

Open Thursday through Monday from 9:00 AM to 5:00 PM. Admission is $2 per person.

Local Tips:

Visit in the morning for cooler weather. Pack a picnic to enjoy in the park's shaded areas.

Cape Romano

109. The Dome Houses of Cape Romano

Location: Cape Romano, South Florida

Address: Accessible by boat from Marco Island, FL

Description:

The Dome Houses of Cape Romano are a fascinating architectural oddity. Built in the 1980s as a self-sustaining home, these partially submerged domes now serve as a striking landmark and a symbol of nature reclaiming its space.

Activities and Attractions:

Take a boat tour to view the domes, snorkel in the surrounding waters, or explore nearby islands. Many tours include fascinating insights into the domes' history and engineering.

Practical Information:

Tours typically cost around $50 per person. The site is only accessible by boat, so plan accordingly.

Local Tips:

Visit during low tide for the best view of the domes. Bring a waterproof camera to capture this unique attraction.

Ellenton

110. Madira Bickel Mound State Archaeological Site

Location: Ellenton, Central Florida

Address: 3708 Patten Ave, Ellenton, FL 34222

Description:

Madira Bickel Mound is an ancient Native American ceremonial site dating back over 2,000 years. It's Florida's first state archaeological site, preserving an important piece of the region's history.

Activities and Attractions:

Walk the short trail to the mound, read interpretive signs detailing its history, and enjoy the serene surroundings of this small but significant site.

Practical Information:

Open daily from 8:00 AM to sunset. Admission is free.

Local Tips:

Combine your visit with a trip to nearby Gamble Plantation Historic State Park for a deeper dive into Florida's history.

Bradenton

111. De Soto National Memorial

Location: Bradenton, Central Florida

Address: 8300 De Soto Memorial Hwy, Bradenton, FL 34209

Description:

De Soto National Memorial commemorates the landing of Spanish explorer Hernando de Soto in 1539. The park blends historical education with scenic natural beauty.

Activities and Attractions:

Explore trails through mangrove forests, visit the visitor center for exhibits on De Soto's expedition, and attend living history demonstrations.

Practical Information:

Open daily from 9:00 AM to 5:00 PM. Admission is free.

Local Tips:

Visit in winter for cooler weather and fewer mosquitoes. Bring comfortable walking shoes for the trails.

Ona

112. Solomon's Castle

Location: Ona, South Florida

Address: 4533 Solomon Rd, Ona, FL 33865

Description:

Solomon's Castle is a whimsical, castle-like structure built entirely from recycled materials by artist Howard Solomon. This shiny, quirky landmark houses an eclectic art collection.

Activities and Attractions:

Take a guided tour of the castle, explore the art gallery, and enjoy a meal at the Boat-in-the-Moat restaurant.

Practical Information:

Open Tuesday through Sunday. Tours cost $10 per person. Parking is free.

Local Tips:

Bring a camera for capturing the castle's unique exterior. Plan to stay for lunch to complete your visit.

Micanopy

113. Micanopy Historic District

Location: Micanopy, North Florida

Address: Cholokka Blvd, Micanopy, FL 32667

Description:

Micanopy Historic District is a charming small-town treasure with antique shops, historic buildings, and a quiet, laid-back atmosphere. Known as Florida's "oldest inland town," it's steeped in history.

Activities and Attractions:

Stroll along Cholokka Blvd to explore unique shops and cafes. Visit the Micanopy Historical Society Museum to learn about the town's rich past.

Practical Information:

Free to explore and open year-round. Parking is available along the main street.

Local Tips:

Visit during the annual Fall Harvest Festival for a lively atmosphere with local crafts, food, and music.

Cape Romano

Sunset sky over the Cape Romano dome house ruins in the Gulf Coast of Florida

Shutterstock / SunflowerMomma

Hidden Gems Deep Dive

UNIQUE AND CURIOUS SPOTS

Dunedin

114. Honeymoon Island Pet Beach

Location: Dunedin, Central Florida

Address: 1 Causeway Blvd, Dunedin, FL 34698

Description:

Honeymoon Island Pet Beach is a dog-friendly haven where you and your furry friend can enjoy soft sands, gentle waves, and scenic Gulf views. It's the perfect spot for a relaxing beach day with your pet.

Activities and Attractions:

Let your dog run along the shoreline or splash in the water. Enjoy a picnic in the designated areas or explore nearby nature trails within Honeymoon Island State Park.

Practical Information:

Open daily from 8:00 AM to sunset. Admission is $8 per vehicle. Dogs must remain leashed and are only allowed in designated areas.

Local Tips:

Visit early in the morning for cooler temperatures and fewer crowds. Bring fresh water and waste bags for your pet's comfort.

Estero

115. The Old Corkscrew Golf Club

Location: Estero, South Florida

Address: 17320 Corkscrew Rd, Estero, FL 33928

Description:

The Old Corkscrew Golf Club is a Jack Nicklaus Signature Course nestled in a serene natural setting. It offers challenging play and breathtaking views for golf enthusiasts.

Activities and Attractions:

Tee off on this meticulously designed 18-hole course surrounded by lush forests and wetlands. The course is renowned for its strategic layout and pristine greens.

Practical Information:

Open daily. Green fees vary by season, starting at $100. Advance reservations are recommended.

Local Tips:

Bring extra balls and your A-game, as this course is known for its difficulty. Enjoy a meal or drink at the clubhouse after your round.

Riviera Beach

116. Peanut Island

Location: Riviera Beach, South Florida

Address: Accessible by water taxi or private boat from Riviera Beach Marina

Description:

Peanut Island is a hidden gem offering clear waters, sandy beaches, and a rich history, including a Cold War-era bunker built for President Kennedy.

Activities and Attractions:

Snorkel in crystal-clear waters, kayak around the island, or take a tour of the historic bunker. The island also features picnic areas and scenic walking trails.

Practical Information:

Open daily, with water taxi rides starting at $15 per person. Admission to the island is free.

Local Tips:

Visit during weekdays for fewer crowds and bring snorkeling gear to explore the vibrant marine life.

Seaside

117. Seaside Scenic Town

Location: Seaside, North Florida

Address: Seaside, FL 32459

Description:

Seaside is a picturesque coastal town known for its pastel-colored cottages, white sand beaches, and vibrant community vibe. It's a perfect destination for a relaxing getaway.

Activities and Attractions:

Stroll through the charming town square, browse unique boutiques, and enjoy dining at locally owned restaurants. Relax on the beach or rent a bike to explore the scenic area.

Practical Information:

Open year-round. Parking is free but can be limited during peak times. Most activities are free to explore, though rentals and dining are additional.

Local Tips:

Visit the iconic "Truman House," featured in The Truman Show. Sunrise and sunset walks on the beach are a must for stunning views.

Part 3

Thematic Itineraries

PLANNING THE ULTIMATE FAMILY GETAWAY?

This section is tailored to families of all sizes, with itineraries designed to entertain and engage kids of all ages. From toddlers to teens, there's something for everyone to enjoy.

What to expect: Explore interactive attractions, discover fun-filled parks, and unwind in safe natural spaces perfect for play and relaxation. These experiences blend adventure and convenience, ensuring a stress-free vacation for parents and unforgettable memories for the entire family.

Family-Friendly Adventures

1-Day Itinerary

Morning: Start your day with an interactive or educational attraction to spark curiosity and engage young minds. For example, visit the **Turtle Hospital in Marathon** to learn about sea turtle conservation or explore the **Florida Caverns State Park** for a guided cave tour filled with awe-inspiring formations.

Lunch Break: Pause for a family-friendly meal at a local gem or a scenic picnic spot. In Marathon, try the on-site café at Robbie's Marina for fresh seafood, or pack a picnic to enjoy at **Blue Spring State Park** with its shaded tables and tranquil views.

Afternoon: Unwind with a fun and relaxing activity. Head to **Honeymoon Island Pet Beach** for some beach time with your furry friends, or enjoy kayaking through the mangroves at **John Pennekamp Coral Reef State Park** for a peaceful adventure.

Final Tips:

Arrive at your morning destination early to maximize your time and beat the crowds.

Pack sunscreen, water, and snacks for the day to stay comfortable and prepared.

Use a map or Google Maps to plan efficient travel routes between stops, ensuring a stress-free day.

3-Day Itinerary

Day 1: Cultural and Educational Attractions

Morning: Start your trip with a visit to the **De Soto National Memorial in Bradenton**, where kids can learn about history through interactive exhibits and scenic trails. Alternatively, explore the **Micanopy Historic District**, rich in history and charming antique shops.

Lunch Break: Dine at a family-friendly restaurant nearby. In Bradenton, try a local seafood spot with outdoor seating for a relaxed meal.

Afternoon: Visit **Solomon's Castle in Ona**, a whimsical landmark that kids will adore for its unique design and art collections. Enjoy a guided tour and have a snack at the Boat-in-the-Moat restaurant.

Day 2: Outdoor Adventures and Nature

Morning: Head to **Blue Spring State Park** in Orange City to enjoy a swim or kayak ride in its crystal-clear waters. During manatee season, observe these gentle giants from the boardwalk.

Lunch Break: Have a picnic at the park or dine at a nearby café with kid-friendly options.

Afternoon: Spend the afternoon hiking or biking through the trails at **Big Shoals State Park in White Springs**, where the whole family can marvel at Florida's largest whitewater rapids.

Day 3: Leisure and Local Fun

Morning: Explore the scenic town of **Seaside**, with its pastel-colored cottages and family-friendly shops. Stroll through the town square and grab breakfast at a cozy café.

Lunch Break: Enjoy a casual family meal in Seaside, with plenty of options for outdoor dining and local treats.

Afternoon: Relax on the sandy shores of **Honeymoon Island Pet Beach** or embark on a short boat tour around **Peanut Island** in Riviera Beach to cap off your trip with some water fun.

Practical Tips:

Accommodations: Opt for family-friendly hotels or vacation rentals with kitchenettes to make mealtime easier.

Transportation: Rent a car for flexibility and convenience when visiting multiple destinations.

Packing Essentials: Bring comfortable clothing, swim gear, and entertainment for the kids during travel time.

7-Day Itinerary

Day 1: Historic St. Augustine

Morning: Begin your journey at the **St. Augustine Historic District**. Wander its cobblestone streets and visit landmarks like the **Castillo de San Marcos**, where kids will love the interactive exhibits and live historical reenactments. Don't miss the pirate-themed attractions for a fun twist on history.

Lunch: Dine at a family-friendly café offering outdoor seating and kid-friendly menus. **Local tip:** Try a spot with views of the historic district for an immersive experience.

Afternoon: Visit **Fort Clinch State Park** and explore its Civil War-era fort, scenic trails, and bike paths. Enjoy beautiful views of the water while learning about the region's history.

Day 2: More Historic Adventures

Morning: Continue exploring St. Augustine with a visit to the **Pirate and Treasure Museum** or take a scenic trolley tour around the city's most iconic spots.

Lunch: Stop by a local diner or seafood shack for fresh, casual dining.

Afternoon: Visit the **Alligator Farm Zoological Park**, where kids can see native reptiles and enjoy hands-on exhibits. For a scenic end to the day, visit the **St. Augustine Lighthouse** for panoramic views.

Day 3: Everglades Exploration

Morning: Head to **Everglades National Park** and join a family-friendly airboat tour through the mangroves. Spot alligators, birds, and other wildlife. For active families, explore **Shark Valley** by bike or tram.

Lunch: Pack a picnic to enjoy in the park or grab lunch at a local restaurant known for fresh seafood and casual meals.

Afternoon: Visit the **Big Cypress National Preserve** for a short nature walk or wildlife spotting.

Day 4: Coral Reefs and Marine Life

Morning: Drive to **John Pennekamp Coral Reef State Park** in Key Largo. Choose between snorkeling, kayaking, or a family-friendly glass-bottom boat tour to see the colorful marine life.

Lunch: Enjoy a picnic by the water or visit a nearby café offering local seafood.

Afternoon: Relax at a nearby beach, letting the kids play in the sand and shallow waters.

Day 5: Theme Park Fun at LEGOLAND

Morning: Spend the entire day at **LEGOLAND Florida Resort**, where kids can enjoy interactive rides, themed exhibits, and the water park. There's something for all ages, from LEGO-building zones to thrilling roller coasters.

Lunch: Dine at one of LEGOLAND's themed restaurants for a fun, whimsical meal.

Afternoon: Continue exploring LEGOLAND, making sure to hit the water attractions if it's a warm day.

Day 6: Gators and Thrills

Morning: Visit **Gatorland** in Orlando and see Florida's famous reptiles up close. Kids can watch live shows, feed the gators, or explore the adventure playground.

Lunch: Enjoy a casual meal at Gatorland's snack bars or nearby family restaurants.

Afternoon: For thrill-seeking teens, try the **Screamin' Gator Zip Line** over the park. Alternatively, visit a nearby nature park to unwind.

Day 7: Relaxation and Memories

Morning: Unwind at **Siesta Key Beach**, famous for its powdery white sands and calm waters. It's perfect for swimming, building sandcastles, or simply relaxing under the sun.

Lunch: Enjoy a laid-back meal at a beachside café or have a picnic under the palm trees.

Afternoon: Head to **Seaside Scenic Town**, where you can browse local boutiques and souvenir shops. Wrap up your trip with ice cream or take a sunset walk along the beach to savor your final moments in Florida.

Tips for Customization:

For younger kids: Add more interactive and hands-on activities, like visiting the **Turtle Hospital** or focusing on calm beaches with shallow waters.

For teens: Include adventurous activities like zip-lining at Gatorland or snorkeling at the **Florida Keys Wreck Trail**.

For a slower pace: Build in downtime with poolside afternoons or extra visits to local parks to keep the itinerary manageable and relaxing.

General Tips for Families

Budget-Friendly Tips:

Save on park visits by purchasing annual passes for state parks or combo tickets for attractions.

Look for discounts online or through local visitor centers. Many attractions offer reduced rates for families or during off-peak times.

Opt for picnic lunches and grocery store snacks instead of dining out for every meal.

Pack Like a Pro:

Bring essentials like reusable water bottles, sunscreen, hats, and comfortable walking shoes.

Pack light snacks, such as granola bars or fruit, to keep kids energized throughout the day.

Don't forget entertainment for downtime, like coloring books, tablets, or portable games.

Timing Is Everything:

Arrive at popular attractions as soon as they open to avoid crowds and long waits.

Plan outdoor activities in the morning or late afternoon to avoid the midday heat.

Check attraction schedules in advance for special events, shows, or seasonal hours.

Romantic Getaways

Looking for the perfect blend of relaxation, adventure, and emotional connection? This section is designed for couples seeking unforgettable moments in Florida's most picturesque settings. Whether you're celebrating an anniversary, planning a honeymoon, or just enjoying a getaway together, these destinations will set the stage for romance.

What to expect: Indulge in intimate candlelit dinners, watch breathtaking sunsets hand-in-hand, take tranquil strolls along pristine beaches, or retreat to charming boutique hotels that feel like your private sanctuary. These experiences are carefully curated to create cherished memories with your special someone.

1-Day Itinerary

Morning: Begin your day with a serene walk or tranquil experience. Visit the **Blowing Rocks Preserve in Jupiter**, where you can stroll hand-in-hand along the beach and admire the dramatic limestone formations. Alternatively, enjoy a peaceful morning at **Harry P. Leu Gardens in Orlando**, exploring the lush, themed gardens.

Lunch Break: Savor a romantic meal at a cozy café or restaurant. For a waterfront view, try the **Columbia Restaurant in St. Augustine**, known for its Spanish charm and intimate ambiance. If you prefer something more casual, a picnic at **Siesta Key Beach** provides both romance and relaxation.

Afternoon: Engage in an intimate or inspiring activity. Take a sunset boat tour in **Key Largo**, where you can watch the sun dip below the horizon. Alternatively, visit **Pewabic Pottery** to explore unique handmade ceramics and pick out a meaningful souvenir together.

Final Tips:

Consider gifting a small token of appreciation, such as a handpicked seashell or a piece of locally crafted jewelry.

End the day with a handwritten note or a spontaneous photo session to capture the moment.

Plan for quiet moments to reflect and reconnect—sometimes the simplest gestures create the most memorable experiences.

3-Day Itinerary

Day 1: Urban Charm and Atmosphere

Morning: Start your getaway with a visit to **St. Augustine Historic District**, where cobblestone streets, historic landmarks, and charming shops set the perfect tone for romance. Explore the **Castillo de San Marcos** for a touch of history.

Lunch Break: Enjoy a leisurely meal at a romantic bistro like the **Ice Plant Bar**, known for its creative cocktails and farm-to-table cuisine.

Afternoon: Take a scenic horse-drawn carriage ride through the historic streets or enjoy a relaxing cruise along the Matanzas River.

Day 2: Natural Wonders and Serenity

Morning: Head to **Blue Spring State Park**, where you can paddle through crystal-clear waters surrounded by lush landscapes. During manatee season, enjoy observing these gentle creatures up close.

Lunch Break: Pack a picnic and dine in the serene surroundings of the park's shaded areas, or visit a nearby café for a light, fresh meal.

Afternoon: Visit **Big Shoals State Park** in White Springs for a quiet hike, taking in views of Florida's largest whitewater rapids. This secluded spot offers a tranquil escape perfect for reconnecting with nature and each other.

Day 3: Leisure and Romantic Farewells

Morning: Spend your final day at **Siesta Key Beach**, known for its powdery white sands and calm waters. Enjoy a leisurely morning walk along the shoreline.

Lunch Break: Dine at a beachfront restaurant with breathtaking views, such as **Ophelia's on the Bay**, offering fresh seafood and an intimate setting.

Afternoon: Explore the charming shops of **Seaside**, picking out a meaningful souvenir or enjoying a quiet moment at a local café. End your trip with a sunset walk on the beach.

Practical Tips:

Accommodations: Opt for boutique hotels, bed & breakfasts, or beachside resorts for a more intimate experience. Consider options like **The Collector Luxury Inn & Gardens** in St. Augustine or a cozy cabin near state parks.

Transportation: Rent a convertible or a luxury car to add a touch of adventure and style to your journey.

Packing Essentials: Bring comfortable yet stylish clothing, a camera to capture memories, and any special items to surprise your partner.

7-Day Itinerary

Days 1-2: Historical and Cultural Atmosphere

Morning: Begin in **St. Augustine Historic District**, wandering its cobblestone streets, historic sites, and charming boutiques. Tour the **Lightner Museum** and savor a lunch at the romantic **Casa Monica Hotel** restaurant.

Afternoon: Explore the **Castillo de San Marcos**, then take a scenic cruise on the Matanzas River for a picturesque sunset view.

Days 3-4: Nature and Adventure

Morning: Discover **Everglades National Park**, taking an intimate airboat tour to see wildlife and enjoy the tranquility of nature.

Lunch Break: Pack a picnic or dine at a local restaurant near the park.

Afternoon: Head to **John Pennekamp Coral Reef State Park** for snorkeling or a glass-bottom boat tour, ideal for couples seeking adventure together.

Days 5-6: Unique and Curious Moments

Morning: Visit the quirky **Solomon's Castle** in Ona, where art and whimsy collide. Take a guided tour of the castle and gardens.

Lunch Break: Enjoy a casual meal at the on-site restaurant, the Boat-in-the-Moat.

Afternoon: Explore the serene beauty of **Blowing Rocks Preserve** in Jupiter, where you can stroll along the beach and admire the dramatic limestone formations.

Day 7: Elegant Farewell

Morning: Unwind at **Siesta Key Beach**, taking in the soft sands and gentle waves.

Lunch Break: Savor a luxurious meal at **The Ritz-Carlton's Jack Dusty** in Sarasota, known for its waterfront views and refined cuisine.

Afternoon: End your trip with a peaceful gondola ride in **Venice**, a perfect farewell to your romantic journey.

Practical Tips:

Accommodations: Choose boutique hotels, charming inns, or luxury resorts like **The Don CeSar** in St. Pete Beach or the **Casa Marina Key West**.

Transportation: Rent a car to explore with ease and flexibility.

Packing Essentials: Bring elegant outfits for fine dining, comfortable attire for nature excursions, and a journal to document your memorable moments together.

General Tips for Romantic Getaways

Choosing the Perfect Stay:

Opt for boutique hotels, lakefront resorts, or unique accommodations to enhance the romance.

Example: "Book a suite at the Grand Hotel on Mackinac Island for a fairy-tale-like stay."

Ideal Timing:

Plan your getaway around seasons that elevate the experience. Spring offers blooming flowers, autumn provides stunning foliage, and summer is perfect for lake activities.

Gifts and Surprises:

Add thoughtful touches to make the trip extra special. Consider arranging a romantic picnic, a private wine tasting, or leaving small surprises like love notes or locally made chocolates for your partner.

Example: "Surprise your partner with a sunset picnic overlooking the shores of Key Largo."

Cultural and Historic Road Trips

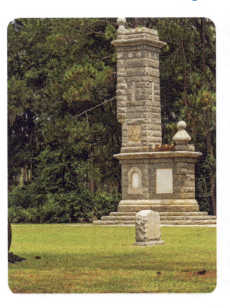

Curious about Florida's rich history and vibrant culture? This section is crafted for travelers eager to dive deep into the stories, traditions, and heritage that shape the Sunshine State. Each itinerary is designed to connect you with the soul of the region.

1-Day Trip

What to expect: Engage in immersive educational experiences, visit interactive museums, and uncover local traditions through guided tours and cultural festivals. From historic landmarks to hidden gems, these journeys promise to enlighten and inspire your inner historian.

Morning: Start your day at the **Castillo de San Marcos** in St. Augustine, the oldest masonry fort in the continental United States. Explore the rich history of this iconic landmark, with engaging ranger-led tours and stunning views of Matanzas Bay. Plan to spend about 2 hours here to fully appreciate its exhibits and scenic surroundings. Parking is available nearby at the city parking garage, a short walk from the site.

Lunch Break: Enjoy a meal at **The Floridian**, a beloved local spot known for its fresh, Southern-inspired dishes with a modern twist. Located just a few blocks from the fort, it's a convenient and delicious choice for recharging before the afternoon.

Afternoon: Head to the **Lightner Museum**, housed in the stunning former Alcazar Hotel. This museum offers a fascinating collection of art, antiques, and relics from the Gilded Age. Allocate around 1.5 to 2 hours to wander through its elegant halls. Parking is available on-site or along nearby streets.

Practical Tips:

Timing: Start your morning at 9:00 AM to make the most of the day and avoid crowds.

Parking: Use the Historic Downtown Parking Facility for easy access to both locations.

What to Bring: Comfortable shoes for walking, as both attractions are within a historic district with cobblestone streets.

3-Day Trip

Day 1: Dive into Urban Culture

Morning: Start your journey in **Miami**, exploring the **Vizcaya Museum and Gardens**, a magnificent early-20th-century estate showcasing Italian Renaissance-inspired architecture and lush gardens. Allow about 2-3 hours to tour the estate and enjoy the serene waterfront views. Parking is available on-site.

Afternoon: Head to **Little Havana** for lunch at **Versailles Restaurant**, a local favorite for authentic Cuban cuisine. Afterward, stroll along Calle Ocho to admire colorful street art, visit cigar shops, and soak in the vibrant culture. Don't miss the **Cuban Memorial Boulevard Park** for a quick history lesson.

Day 2: Explore Rural History

Morning: Drive to **Micanopy**, a charming small town rich in history. Begin your day at the **Micanopy Historical Society Museum**, where you'll learn about the area's Native American and pioneer heritage. Allow 1-1.5 hours for this visit. Parking is free and plentiful.

Afternoon: After a hearty lunch at **Pearl Country Store & BBQ**, visit **Paynes Prairie Preserve State Park**, a National Natural Landmark. Walk the boardwalk or hike the trails to spot wild bison and horses, immersing yourself in Florida's rural past. Spend 2-3 hours here before returning to town.

Day 3: End with a Scenic Road Trip

Morning: Set off along **Florida's Scenic Highway A1A**, a route lined with historic sites and breathtaking coastal views. Stop at the **Fort Matanzas National Monument**, a historic Spanish fort dating back to 1742. Spend about 1-2 hours exploring and enjoying the trails. Parking is free.

Afternoon: Conclude your trip in **St. Augustine**, the nation's oldest city. Visit the **St. Augustine Lighthouse & Maritime Museum** for stunning views and a fascinating look at maritime history. Allocate 2-3 hours here. Wrap up your day with a leisurely dinner in the historic district at **Collage Restaurant**, known for its intimate ambiance and globally inspired menu.

Practical Tips:

Timing: Start each day early (around 9:00 AM) to avoid crowds and maximize your time.

Transportation: A car is essential for this itinerary; plan for a mix of highways and scenic roads.

Packing Essentials: Comfortable walking shoes, sunscreen, and a camera to capture the picturesque locations.

7-Day Trip

Day 1 - Miami:

Morning: Start at the **Perez Art Museum Miami (PAMM)** to explore contemporary art with a focus on Latin America. Spend about 2 hours here, then take a stroll through the adjacent Museum Park.

Afternoon: Visit **Little Havana** for lunch at **Versailles Restaurant** and enjoy the vibrant culture of Calle Ocho. End your day at **Wynwood Walls**, Miami's iconic open-air street art museum.

Day 2 - Tampa:

Morning: Explore the **Henry B. Plant Museum**, located in a former luxury hotel and filled with Victorian opulence. Spend about 1-2 hours here.

Afternoon: Visit **Ybor City**, Tampa's historic district, to learn about its cigar-making heritage and enjoy authentic Cuban cuisine at **Columbia Restaurant**.

Day 3 - St. Augustine:

Morning: Start at the **Castillo de San Marcos**, the oldest masonry fort in the U.S. Plan for 2 hours to explore the exhibits and scenic views.

Afternoon: Head to the **St. Augustine Pirate & Treasure Museum** for an interactive dive into maritime history. Allocate 1.5 hours here.

Day 4 - Rural Florida:

Morning: Drive to **Micanopy**, a charming town with deep historical roots. Visit the **Micanopy Historical Society Museum** to learn about Native American and pioneer history.

Afternoon: Stop by **Paynes Prairie Preserve State Park** for a guided hike or wildlife viewing, immersing yourself in Florida's natural beauty.

Day 5 - Florida Keys:

Morning: Visit the **Ernest Hemingway Home and Museum** in Key West to explore the life of the literary legend. Spend about 1.5 hours here.

Afternoon: Head to the **Key West Shipwreck Museum**, offering a fascinating look at the region's maritime history.

Day 6 - Orlando:

Morning: Discover **Leu Gardens**, a historic botanical garden with scenic walking paths.

Afternoon: Visit the **Orlando Science Center**, featuring engaging exhibits for visitors of all ages.

Day 7: Historic Charm in Pensacola

Morning: Explore **Historic Pensacola Village**, a collection of restored homes and buildings from the 19th century. Plan for 2-3 hours to fully enjoy the guided tours and exhibits.

Afternoon: End your trip at the **National Naval Aviation Museum**, a world-class museum showcasing aircraft and naval history.

Practical Tips:

Transportation: A car is essential for this itinerary, with multiple cities and regions to explore.

Timing: Start each day early to maximize your visits and avoid crowds.

Packing Essentials: Comfortable walking shoes, sunscreen, and a notebook for jotting down interesting historical facts.

General Tips for a Cultural and Historical Road Trip

Choosing the Right Vehicle

Opt for a **spacious and comfortable car** that's well-suited for long drives with multiple stops. A midsize SUV or minivan is ideal for accommodating luggage, souvenirs, and passengers, while providing a smooth ride on highways and scenic routes.

Essential Gear to Bring

Printed Guidebook and Map: While GPS is handy, a printed guide or map adds a layer of reliability, especially in areas with limited cell service.

Themed Playlist: Create a road trip playlist featuring local artists, historical ballads, or instrumental tracks to set the mood for your cultural journey.

Comfort Items: Bring a travel pillow, reusable water bottle, and snacks to stay refreshed and comfortable during longer drives.

Notebook or Journal: Jot down memorable experiences or interesting historical tidbits from your stops.

Ideal Stop Durations

To fully appreciate each site, plan to spend:

1-2 hours for smaller museums, landmarks, or walking tours.

2-3 hours for more complex sites like large museums, state parks, or historic districts.

This allows ample time to explore, take photos, and enjoy the experience without feeling rushed.

Additional Tips:

Start early to make the most of daylight hours.

Research parking availability at each site to avoid delays.

Incorporate breaks for scenic stops or local eateries to enhance your trip.

Alphabetical Index

A

Amelia Island Beaches
Apalachicola Historic District
Art Deco Historic District
Anna Maria Island Beaches

B

Big Pine Key (Key Deer Refuge)
Big Talbot Island (Boneyard Beach)
Big Shoals State Park
Blackwater River State Forest
Blowing Rocks Preserve
Bok Tower Gardens
Boynton Beach Oceanfront Park

C

Caladesi Island State Park
Cape Romano Dome Houses
Cape San Blas Beaches
Castillo de San Marcos National Monument
Cedar Key Beaches
Cedar Key Museum State Park
Cedar Lakes Woods and Gardens
Cayo Costa State Park
Crystal River (Swim with Manatees)
Coral Gables Venetian Pool

D

De Leon Springs (Old Spanish Sugar Mill)
De Soto National Memorial
DeLand's Stetson Mansion
Devil's Den Prehistoric Spring
Devil's Millhopper Geological State Park
Dog Island
Dry Tortugas National Park
Dunedin Honeymoon Island Pet Beach

E

Edison and Ford Winter Estates
Egmont Key State Park
Ernest Hemingway House
Everglades National Park

F

Falling Waters State Park
Fakahatchee Strand Preserve State Park
Fernandina Beach Historic District
Fort Clinch State Park
Fort Lauderdale's Las Olas Boulevard
Fort Myers Beach
Fort Zachary Taylor Historic State Park

G

Gatorland
Gainesville Devil's Millhopper Geological State Park
Gasparilla Island
Grayton Beach State Park
Gulf Islands National Seashore

H

Harry P. Leu Gardens
Hollywood Beach Broadwalk
Homosassa Three Sisters Springs

I

Islamorada (Sportfishing Capital)
Islamorada Robbie's Marina (Feed the Tarpon)

J

John Pennekamp Coral Reef State Park
Jupiter Blowing Rocks Preserve

K

Key Biscayne Lighthouse
Key Largo Coral Reef State Park
Key West and Mallory Square

L

Lake Placid Murals
Little Torch Key (Secluded Escape)
Lover's Key State Park
Long Key State Park

M

Manatee Springs State Park
Marco Island Beaches
Marathon's Turtle Hospital
Marianna Florida Caverns State Park
Matlacha Art District
Merritt Island Wildlife Refuge
Miami Beach and South Beach
Micanopy Historic District
Milton Blackwater River State Forest
Mount Dora Downtown
Mount Dora Scenic Boat Tours

N

Naples Botanical Garden
Naples Pier and Beaches
Navarre Beach

O

Ocala National Forest
Ona Solomon's Castle
Orlando Universal Studios Florida

P

Peacock Springs State Park
Pensacola Beach
Pensacola Lighthouse and Museum
Perdido Key

R

Rainbow Springs Tubing
Riviera Beach Peanut Island

S

Sarasota Jungle Gardens
Seaside Scenic Town
SeaWorld Orlando
Shark Valley (Everglades Cycling and Tram Tours)
Siesta Key Beach
Silver Springs State Park
Solomon's Castle
St. Augustine Historic District
St. George Island State Park
St. Marks Wildlife Refuge
St. Vincent Island
Sugarloaf Key Bat Tower

T

Tampa Bay History Center
The Dome Houses of Cape Romano
The Ringling Museum of Art
Three Sisters Springs
Torreya State Park

V

Venice Beach (Shark Tooth Capital)

W

Wakulla Springs State Park
Walt Disney World Resort
White Springs Big Shoals State Park
Winter Park Scenic Boat Tour

Enjoyed This Guide? Your Review Helps!

Hey there, traveler!

If this book helped you **discover Florida's best spots, plan a smoother trip, or uncover a hidden gem you wouldn't have found otherwise**, I'd love to hear about it! **Your review makes a big difference**—not just for me, but for other travelers searching for a guide that truly helps them make the most of their time in the Sunshine State.

Leaving a review is quick and easy—just scan the **QR code at the end of this book**, and you'll be taken straight to the review page. Even a few words about what you found most useful can go a long way! And if you want to **help future readers even more**, consider **adding a photo or video of the inside pages**—it's the best way to show them exactly what to expect.

Thanks for your support, and enjoy every moment of your Florida adventure!

Unlock Your Free Bonuses!

Hey there, traveler!

Before you close this book, don't forget to **grab the exclusive bonuses** that come with it! They're designed to **enhance your Florida adventure** and make planning even easier. And the best part? **They're completely free!**

Accessing them is simple—just scan the **QR code at the end of this book**, and you'll be taken directly to the download page. No complicated steps, no extra hassle—just instant access to the extra resources waiting for you.

Enjoy your trip, and happy exploring!

https://drive.google.com/drive/folders/1oEdHSF2z56tBYRIfF8iayqDA-k70uMJLT?usp=sharing

Made in United States
North Haven, CT
12 July 2025

70598246R10065